P9-DBP-389

The Threat
from
Within

The Threat from Within

*Unethical
Politics and
Politicians*

*by Michael
Kronenwetter*

*Franklin Watts
New York
London
Toronto
Sydney
1986*

Photographs and cartoons courtesy of Norris-Vancouver Sun, Canada/ Rothco Cartoons: p. 13; Liederman-L.I. Press, NY/Rothco Cartoons: p. 16; © Robert Dornfried/Rothco Cartoons: p. 22; UPI/Bettmann Newsphotos: pp. 24, 60, 88, 110; Larry Stevens/Photo Trends: p. 25; © 1972, Paul Conrad for the Los Angeles Times, Los Angeles Times Syndicate, reprinted with permission: p. 27; AP/Wide World: pp. 32, 34, 45, 46; © 1978, Paul Conrad for The Los Angeles Times, Los Angeles Times Syndicate, reprinted with permission: p. 54; Dennis Renault-Sacramento Bee, CA/Rothco Cartoons: p. 58; © 1983, Paul Conrad for The Los Angeles Times, Los Angeles Times Syndicate, reprinted with permission: pp. 59, 118; Konopacki/Rothco Cartoons: p. 66; Jim Mazzotta-Ft. Myers News-Press, FL/Rothco Cartoons: p. 69; Sidney Harris: pp. 77, 104; © Punch/Rothco Cartoons: p. 94; © 1970, Paul Conrad for The Los Angeles Times, Los Angeles Times Syndicate, reprinted with permission: p. 102.

Library of Congress Cataloging-in-Publication Data

Kronenwetter, Michael.
The threat from within.

Bibliography: p.
Includes index.
Summary: Discusses the issue of ethics in political conduct with examples of dirty campaign tricks, voter fraud, and campaign lies drawn from United States' history.
1. Elections—United States—Corrupt practices—History—Juvenile literature. 2. Corruption (in politics)—United States—History—Juvenile literature. [1. Elections—United States—Corrupt practices—History. 2. Corruption (in politics)]
I. Title.
JK1994.K76 1986   324.973   86-11122
ISBN 0-531-10252-1

Contents

*The Threat
from
Within*

1

Ethics
and
Politics

The Concept of Ethics

According to a typical dictionary definition, ethics is the study of "standards of conduct and moral judgment." Ethics, then, has to do with conduct—with the way people behave. And it judges that conduct by moral standards. It is primarily concerned not with the *wisdom* of political actions but with their morality.

At its most basic, ethical behavior is what we usually think of as good behavior, while unethical behavior is what we usually think of as bad. Political behavior, like other behavior, has its ethical considerations.

In this book we will look at unethical behavior in American politics, what it is, some of the pressures that cause it, and the harm it can do to the democratic political process and the fundamental principle of representative democracy on which that process is based. We will be concerned not with the partisan goals or political philosophies of individual politicians but with how their actions affect that process.

This is an important distinction. It can be argued that almost any kind of political action, however unethical in itself, might be justified if the political motive for it is noble enough. It is the old argument about whether or not the end justifies the means. Does a good end justify a bad means? If a candidate were running in an election against a modern Hitler, for example, would *any* action taken to defeat him be morally wrong? Wouldn't any strategy, however morally distasteful in itself, be justified if it could have saved the world from the potential evils of such a person?

Such questions reflect serious ethical concerns, but here we will be primarily concerned with means, not with ends. Any political goal can be pursued using either ethical or unethical political practices. We will talk mostly about such practices rather than about the ultimate goals of the politicians involved. We will use examples of unethical practices drawn from Republicans and Democrats alike, as well as from Whigs and Federalists, conservatives and liberals, and others with no political philosophy at all.

Unethical political behavior comprises those unfair or corrupt practices that conflict with the basic principle of representative democracy or that interfere with the proper functioning of our political system.

Representative Democracy

Our political system is democratic because it assumes that the ultimate authority of the government comes from the people. (The Greek word *demos*, from which *democracy* is derived, means "the people.") But our system is also representative. That is, in America the people do not govern collectively. Instead, we choose individuals to hold public office, to govern us with our permission and in our name. Once American citizens have reached a certain age, we are entitled to take part in the election of those officials. The officials, then, *represent* the citizenry as a whole and are to work in the citizens' behalf to protect our constitutional rights and to promote what the Constitution calls "the general welfare."

This concept of representation is not a simple one. One of the major unresolved political questions of our democracy has to do with the nature of representation. Clearly, elected officials represent their constituents. They represent the people of their district or state, or, in the case of some federal officials like the President, the people of the country as a whole. But what are the limits and obligations of that representation? Are they bound to represent all constituents equally, or do they have a special obligation to that portion of the electorate which voted for them? Some politicians and political scientists would argue each side of that issue.

The question is complicated by the fact that public officials are elected not only to represent their constituents but also to lead them. What should they do, then, when their judgment and that of the majority of the public are in conflict? Should the officials follow their own convictions or those of the people who elected them?

Some politicians believe that a public official is ethically bound by the will of the people. The official should always follow the wishes of the voters, because that is what the voters elected him or her to do. Other politicians argue that the voters chose them for their intelligence, judgment, and integrity, not just for their ability to read public opinion polls. It would be unethical, they believe, for them to act contrary to their own moral judgment simply because a majority of their constituents disagreed with them.

Still others believe that there is no cut-and-dried solution to this dilemma. It is a question that politicians must decide over again in each case as it arises. They must weigh the strength and quality of their own beliefs against those of their constituents, consider the political risk, and then decide.

This debate over the nature of political representation

plays a significant part in the ethical dilemmas that politicians repeatedly face. It is a key element in many of the decisions they are called upon to make.

Politics

The word *politics* is sometimes used in the narrow sense of the business of getting elected to (and staying in) office. We will use it here in its broader sense to mean the process by which our system of representative democracy functions. A politician, then, is anyone involved in that process, whether in public office or out of it.

People seem to have a low opinion of politics and politicians, however you define them. When asked in public opinion polls to rank various professions in the order of how much respect they have for them, most people put politics far down the list, if not at the bottom.

The word itself is often used as a term of contempt. "That's just politics," people say when they want to disparage an activity. "He's just a politician," they say when they mean "hypocrite." As the journalist H. L. Mencken put it, in America the word "politician" is used to mean "a member of a professionally dishonest and dishonorable class. An *honest* politician is regarded as a sort of marvel, comparable to a calf with five legs."

It is as though the profession itself were somehow inherently unethical. But it is not. It is as honorable—and even as noble—a profession as a democracy has to offer, and most politicians do their best to live up to it. Senator Charles Mathias, Jr., probably came closer to the truth than Mencken, when he said of his fellow politicians: "Most of us are honest all the time, and all of us are honest most of the time." Certainly the politician's job is vitally important. It is nothing less than the governing of the country.

Politics is sometimes called a science and sometimes an art. Perhaps most meaningfully, it has been called "the art of the possible." It involves getting things done. Politics is

"I'M MIGHTY SUSPICIOUS OF POLITICIANS WHO DON'T MAKE
WILD PROMISES I CAN COUNT ON THEM NOT KEEPING. . . ."

not an abstract study. It operates in the real world. Roads must be built, laws must be passed, and the courts must function, if the society is to run at all.

It is not enough, then, for a politician to be concerned only with what is right or good, with the way things *should* be. It is the politician's job to *make* things the way they should be, or as close to it as possible. Performing that job often requires compromise. In a complex society such as ours, many different interests must be accommodated. Business and labor, liberals and conservatives, rich and poor, minorities and the majority, the employed and the unemployed, the old and the young—each has its claim on society, and each turns to the government to see that claim fulfilled. It falls to the politician to satisfy them all or to pay the consequences of their anger.

The politicians must find ways to strike a compromise between the real interests of these and other groups—each of which has its own needs, beliefs, and values. In order to get something in the real world of politics, it is usually necessary to give something in return. Inevitably, politicians find that they must compromise some of their own beliefs and values in the process.

In many areas of life, particularly where serious moral questions are involved, compromise itself is often considered unethical. If something is right, people feel, it is right. There should be no compromise. But in government —which means in politics—compromise is absolutely necessary. It is even considered by most American politicians to be a positive good, at least when it is kept within ethical limits.

But setting those limits can be difficult.

The Ethical Code

Ethics is not only the study of "standards of conduct and moral judgment." It is also "the code of morals of a particular profession." It would be convenient if such a code of morals could be drawn up for the political profession, one that would cover all situations and circumstances. But that kind of comprehensive code is impossible to arrive at. The profession of politics is too complex—and too rooted in dilemma and compromise—to lend itself to simple rules and regulations.

Only the most basic elements of such a code are generally agreed upon. We want our politicians to be honest and to put the public's welfare ahead of their private ambition. We do not want them to take bribes or to steal our money.

Those two provisions have even been written into the criminal law. Bribery and embezzlement are not just unethical, they are illegal. This brings up an important distinction.

Ethical and legal are not the same concepts. Whether or not an act is illegal is a matter of law. Is there a law against it? Whether or not an act is unethical is a matter of morals. Is it morally wrong? It is conceivable that a political practice might be unethical without being illegal, or even be illegal without being unethical. In general, however, it can be said that if a political practice is illegal, it is *likely* to be unethical as well. But the reverse is less true. That is, many practices that are perfectly legal are still generally regarded as unethical by politicians and the public alike.

There have been attempts to write more extensive codes of political ethics than those enshrined in the law. Many government agencies, for example, have written codes of ethics for their own employees. None of these have been very successful at curtailing unethical behavior, however. Because so much of political ethics involves intangible elements like motivation and intention, the bulk of any truly effective code of political ethics will have to exist in the minds and consciences of individual politicians, if it is to exist at all.

The world of politics, which is also the world of government, is extremely large and complex. In its many forms,

government reaches into every aspect of our lives. Politicians of all kinds wield enormous power. The stakes are high and the temptations great. They include the temptations to seize political power unfairly, to misuse it, to violate the public trust, and to profit at the public's expense. Unfortunately, many politicians give in to these temptations. They willfully violate the code—written or unwritten—of political ethics.

When they do, we all suffer. Unethical political behavior damages not just individuals but the whole society. Some of that damage is direct and obvious. The evils of bribery, extortion, and vote fraud are apparent to everyone. But there are other forms of unethical politicial behavior whose damage is more subtle. Ultimately, all such behavior damages the fabric of democracy itself. It prevents it from functioning as it was designed to function, in the interests of all the citizens.

In the remaining chapters of this book, we will examine some of the most common forms of unethical political behavior and the damage that they do.

*Winning
at Any Cost*

The First Rule

The first rule of politics is "Get elected."

That might sound like a cynical proposition. It seems unethical to put personal ambition ahead of the public good. But there is nothing unethical about it, as long as it is properly understood.

Elections are the heart's blood of the American political system. The importance placed on them by the people who designed our political system is shown by the fact that elections are called for in the very first article of the U.S. Constitution. Elections are vital to our whole concept of representative democracy because they are the most direct way we have of choosing those who will represent us. They are also the chief remedy we have for irresponsible or unethical behavior on the part of elected officials. They allow us an easy means of removing them from office.

Elections, however, are more than a kind of public employment service. Government officials can be chosen in any of a number of other ways, and many are. So many officials are needed to make our local, state, and federal governments function that electing them all would be impracticable. Furthermore, officials in some positions seem to function better when removed from the immediate political considerations involved in running for election. Consequently many government employees are chosen through civil service tests while even some of our most important officials (such as federal judges) are appointed rather than elected.

Yet even these nonelected officials are subject to the public's will, at least indirectly. They may be appointed to office by an elected official, or they may serve under the authority of an elected official, or both. Even the members of the U.S. Supreme Court, who hold their jobs for life providing they are not guilty of misconduct, are appointed by the (elected) President of the United States, with the approval of the (elected) Senate.

Elections, then, play the primary role in our political process. Only through the consent of the governed does the government derive its authority over us—and only through elections is the consent of the governed given.

For the politician seeking political office, an election is much more than just a way to get a job. It is a kind of political baptism that must be undergone in order to obtain the right to hold political power. And whatever the politician's goals, he or she must obtain political power in order to accomplish them. He or she must *get elected*.

The more important and worthwhile a politician's goals—to promote peace, reform the tax code, help the poor, strengthen the nation's defense system, or whatever—the more important it is for the politician to get elected. In this sense, there is a direct relationship between a politician's desire to do good and his or her personal politicial ambition. There is nothing inherently unethical, then, about a politician's desire to win an election. Winning elections is a large part of what the American political system is all about.

Although "Get elected" is the first rule of politics, it is

not the only one. In order for the system to work as it should, elections must be conducted ethically—according to the principles of honesty and fairness. In order for the consent of the governed to be legitimately given, the voters must have the opportunity to compare the candidates for office, to make informed judgments about the views and character of each one, and finally to choose between them. Ideally, this means that the candidates must present themselves and their positions openly and honestly during the campaign, and that the voting process itself must be conducted with scrupulous honesty.

Actual elections often fall short of this ideal. Many politicians seem to follow the famous dictum usually attributed (falsely) to professional football coach Vince Lombardi: "Winning isn't the most important thing, it's the *only* thing!" In pursuit of election, they have developed a wide range of questionable campaign practices, each designed to give them an unfair advantage over their opponent.

Telling Lies

President Abraham Lincoln once warned that "You may fool all the people some of the time; you can even fool some of the people all the time; but you can't fool all of the people all the time." Despite this famous warning, many politicians continue to do their best to fool the people.

Candidates want to project an "image"—a vision of themselves—that will appeal to the voters. Most people would agree that nothing is unethical about this when the image is intended to be an accurate reflection of the politician and of his or her intentions and beliefs. Even when the image is clearly selective—revealing only what the candidate sees as positive about himself or herself and hiding what is negative—many politicians would argue that they are only following common sense. After all, why should they emphasize their unattractive qualities? Opponents can be relied on to do that.

In some extreme cases, however, the image bears almost no relation to the reality. It is meant not to reveal the candidate in the best possible light but to conceal the candidate. It is designed to make the voters believe things about the candidate that are not true. In effect, it is a kind of elaborate lie, or collection of lies. In the pursuit of a better image, some candidates have misrepresented, among many other things, their military and political records, their ethnic backgrounds, their wealth or lack of it, their education, their work experience, and even their real names and ages.

Politicians routinely misrepresent their family lives. Voters like to believe that elected officials have happy family lives, and many politicians are determined to project that happy-family image whether it is accurate or not. (Until recently it was widely believed that no one who was divorced could ever be elected President.) Few politicians will admit to any domestic strife. It is common for political husbands and wives who rarely speak to each other to pose lovingly for the television cameras. There have been cases of couples campaigning together, presenting an image of domestic bliss to the voters, while secretly meeting with their divorce lawyers. The divorce, of course, was scheduled to take place after the election.

Some candidates even misrepresent their own political beliefs and intentions. Conservative candidates may try to sound more liberal when speaking to liberal-minded voters, while liberal candidates with conservative constituencies may try to sound more conservative. Often they will not lie, in the sense of saying things that are false in themselves, but rather they will make statements that, while true in themselves, leave a false impression. A state legislator, for example, might tell a crowd of gun-control advocates that he voted for a bill which called for the registration of handguns, neglecting to mention that it called only for the registration of handguns with very short barrels. In this way he gives the impression that he supports tough handgun legislation, when in fact he does not.

One of the most serious misrepresentations of this kind occurred during the presidential election campaign of 1964. The incumbent Democratic President, Lyndon Johnson, was being challenged by conservative Republican Senator Barry Goldwater.

American forces were fighting in a relatively small undeclared war in Southeast Asia at the time, on the side of the government of South Vietnam against communist rebels supported by the country of North Vietnam. Here at home, many people were concerned about the war. Some were worried that we were too deeply involved in what they saw as a foreign civil war, and that too many Americans were being killed. Others were worried that we were not involved deeply enough, and that the communists might overrun South Vietnam and continue on to take over all of Southeast Asia.

Not surprisingly, the war became an issue in the election campaign. Goldwater was an announced "hawk." He believed the United States should increase its military involvement in Vietnam and do anything necessary to "defeat communism" there. Since Goldwater already had the support of the hawks, Johnson did everything he could to get the support of the "doves." He presented himself as a peace candidate who intended to pull American forces out of Vietnam. He succeeded, winning reelection in a landslide, capturing the electoral vote in forty-five states.

Almost immediately, President Johnson escalated American military involvement in Vietnam. Within months, he had committed more American troops and widened the war by bombing North Vietnam. By the end of 1965, almost 200,000 Americans were in Southeast Asia, and thousands had already died.

Good evidence suggests that Johnson never intended to de-escalate the war. He was determined not to "lose Vietnam" to the communists. His pose as a "peace candidate" had been a deception on the American voters.

The 1964 presidential campaign took place during the early stages of the Vietnam War. Senator Barry Goldwater (above), a "hawk," ran against the incumbent, Lyndon B. Johnson (right), a "dove." Johnson won the election but wound up escalating the war. There's a good chance that some of the students shown with Johnson either went to war or demonstrated against it.

This was not an isolated instance. Four years later, with American troops still engaged in Vietnam, the Republican presidential candidate Richard Nixon campaigned saying that he had a "secret plan" to end the war in Vietnam. He gave the impression that if he was elected, he would have the war over, at least as far as America was concerned, within months. Nixon did win the election. However, four years later, America was still enmeshed in Vietnam, and tens of thousands more people had died.

Defending Misrepresentations

Politicians offer a number of justifications for such misrepresentations. The couple planning to divorce, for example, might argue that they were under no obligation to reveal their plan to end the marriage. They did not so much mislead the voters as simply fail to inform them. Candidates, after all, cannot possibly reveal *everything* about themselves to the voters, nor should they be required to. In this case, to have revealed their divorce plans would only have meant introducing an irrelevant, but negative, factor into their campaign.

The legislator speaking to the gun-control group might insist that he did in fact vote for that one handgun-registration bill, so he had merely been telling the truth. If the listeners then jumped to the false conclusion that he was a strong gun-control advocate, that was their mistake.

Officeholders have many explanations for failing to keep campaign promises. More often than not, they deny any attempt to mislead the voters. They made the promise in good faith, they argue, but someone or something beyond their control prevented them from keeping it. Circumstances changed, or they could not get enough of their colleagues to go along with them. Sometimes this explanation is true. At other times it is not. Since there is no way to get inside another person's mind, the voter is left with the choice of accepting or rejecting this kind of explanation on faith.

"... Four more years? ... Four more years? ..."

[*This cartoon was published in 1972, after Richard M. Nixon was reelected president. The Vietnam War was still in full swing.*]

Presidents regularly blame Congress for unkept campaign promises. "I *tried* to keep my promise," a President will claim, "but I couldn't get Congress to go along." Those in Congress might respond that if, as President, a candidate would lack the power to fulfill a promise, the candidate should not make the promise in the first place.

Johnson's supporters might claim that, although Johnson did escalate the war, he escalated it less than Goldwater would have done. (Goldwater had suggested the possibility of using nuclear weapons.) Therefore, his stance as a peace candidate was justified—at least in comparison to his opponent.

Both Johnson's and Nixon's supporters might argue that neither of them could afford to be honest about their military and diplomatic plans in regard to the war. That would have been giving away secrets to the enemy. Their critics, on the other hand, might respond that if they could not tell the truth about their plans, they should have said nothing about them at all. Deceiving the enemy is one thing; deceiving the American public is another.

As we have seen, the ethical merits of specific misrepresentations are often arguable. It is not always easy to draw the line between an ethical attempt to appeal to voters and an unethical attempt to deceive them. But that line must be drawn somewhere. It is, after all, only through the consent of the people that politicians receive the authority to act in our name. If the people are, to use Lincoln's word, "fooled" into giving their consent, the legitimacy of that authority is thrown into question.

Smearing the Opposition

A political "smear" is an attempt to damage the reputation of a political opponent, usually by spreading false and malicious information about him or her. It is an old tradition in American politics. The first documented smear in American presidential politics, for example, occurred in the very first contested presidential election, the 1796 race between John Adams and Thomas Jefferson. (The first President, George Washington, had been unopposed.)

A pro-Jefferson newspaper in Boston charged that during the American Revolution Adams had joined a conspiracy to have Washington removed from command of the colonial forces. The charge was untrue. Adams had actually worked to *keep* Washington in command when others tried to dislodge him. But the readers didn't know it was untrue, and although it didn't cost Adams the election, the story hurt him in two ways. First, it made him appear to be an enemy of Washington, who was still a very popular figure. Second, because Adams had always publicly claimed to support Washington, the report made him seem to be both disloyal and a hypocrite.

The smear in this case did not come from the opposing candidate, Jefferson, but from Jefferson's supporters. This is a common practice in political campaigns. Sometimes it is a deliberate tactic. When a charge is going to be made that is either untrue or exceptionally harsh, it is left to someone other than the candidate to make it. That way, if the charge is later proved false, the candidate can deny having had anything to do with it. (Sometimes, a candidate *doesn't* have anything to do with it. Supporters often act on their own, making dubious, even wild, charges without the knowledge of their own candidate.) Such charges occasionally backfire and embarrass the candidate they were intended to help.

Another famous political smear came in the presidential election campaign of 1844. Its victim was the Democratic nominee, James K. Polk. Shortly before the election an Ithaca, New York, newspaper published what it said was an excerpt from the travel diary of a European named Baron Roorback, who had visited the United States in 1836. The excerpt consisted of Roorback's account of a slave auction he claimed to have witnessed. Polk was a bidder, according to Roorback, and bought some forty slaves. Furthermore, he had his initials branded on their skin with a hot iron.

Slavery was legal in the South at that time, but the story of the branding made Polk seem exceptionally cruel, even to other slaveowners. Besides, the paper wasn't printed in the South. It was printed in New York, a key state in the election and one in which there was strong anti-slavery feeling. "Roorback's Journal," as it was called, was a fabrication. Even the name "Baron Roorback" had been made up. The story hurt Polk in New York, but he still carried the state—by about five thousand votes.

A charge does not have to be untrue to be a smear. It only has to be misleading and harmful. A case in point occurred in the 1950 Democratic party primary in Florida. Congressman George Smathers wanted to unseat the incumbent U.S. senator, Claude Pepper. Speaking to uneducated voters, Smathers cleverly managed to smear Pepper by stating misleading "truths" about the senator's family. He described Pepper's sister, for example, as a "thespian" (an actress) and his brother as a "practicing *Homo sapiens*" (human being). The senator, himself, he said, was a "sexagenarian"—which means someone between sixty and sixty-nine years old.

Most of the "charges" were true. None of them should have damaged Pepper's campaign. But they did. To many of the uneducated voters of rural Florida, each implied some kind of sexual misconduct. Pepper lost the primary.

Dirty Tricks

Still another unethical campaign practice is the "dirty trick." In political parlance, a dirty trick is any attempt by a candidate, or that candidate's supporters, to sabotage the opponent's campaign. An early example of a dirty trick took place during the campaign of 1832. President Andrew Jackson was running for re-election, and among those working to defeat him was his bitter enemy Senator Henry Clay of Kentucky. Clay was a powerful man, particularly in his home state, and a formidable campaigner. He was determined to use all his power and ability to turn the voters against Jackson.

Clay was scheduled to make an important speech in Louisville, but on the day of the speech he found himself a long way south of the state capital. He hired a boatman to row him up the Ohio River to the city. Unknown to the senator, the boatman was a Jackson supporter, and when the boat came to the junction of the Ohio and Salt rivers, he rowed up the Salt instead. Clay never got to make his speech, and the phrase "up Salt River" became a part of the political language. To this day it signifies any kind of political defeat.

This was a somewhat unusual dirty trick, in that it was carried out on the spur of the moment, rather than as a part of a premeditated plan. It is unusual, too, in that the trickster was an ordinary citizen, not an active participant in the campaign.

A variation of this speech-preventing maneuver was carried out more than a century later in the California gubernatorial campaign of 1962. Like many other candidates before and since, the Republican candidate, Richard Nixon, conducted a whistle-stop tour as a part of his campaign. That is, he traveled about the country on a special railroad train. The train would stop at the small stations along the way, where the candidate would speak from the back of the train to people gathered on the station platform. The term "whistle stop" came from the old practice of blowing the train's whistle at each stop to attract a crowd.

One day when Nixon was making his usual speech from the back of the last railroad car, the train jerked to a start in the middle of it and pulled out of the station, removing the shocked candidate in midsentence. It turned out that a man named Dick Tuck, working for the Democrats, had dressed up as a station man and signaled the engineer—who couldn't see Nixon at the rear of the train—that it was time to leave.

Tuck is widely recognized as the master of this kind

*Nixon on a whistle-stop tour during the 1962
California gubernatorial campaign*

of cheerful, high-spirited dirty trick. On one occasion, when Nixon gave a speech in Los Angeles's Chinatown, a neighborhood populated mostly by Chinese-Americans, Tuck arranged for a large sign to be hung behind the candidate. The sign was printed in both English and Chinese. The English words were a message of welcome, and Nixon apparently assumed that the Chinese characters were a translation. He was delighted with the sign, and even asked to have his picture taken, smiling and waving, in front of it.

As those in the crowd who read Chinese were aware, however, the Chinese words were anything but friendly. They were in fact a hostile political message dictated by Tuck. When the picture was printed in several newspapers and the actual translation of the message was made public, Nixon was highly embarrassed.

In the 1972 presidential campaign, the Nixon forces decided to take a leaf from their old enemy's book. They launched a dirty-trick campaign of their own against the Democrats.

This campaign was headed by a young man named Donald Segretti. Some of the tricks Segretti and his staff pulled were as high-spirited and humorous as Tuck's usually were. When one of the candidates for the Democratic presidential nomination held a large fund-raising dinner in Washington, Segretti's dirty tricksters enjoyed themselves enormously. They ordered all kinds of expensive articles sent to the dinner and had the bills sent to the Democratic candidate. As an extra touch, they sent invitations to sixteen ambassadors from foreign nations, disguising the fact that the dinner was a campaign fund-raiser, since ambassadors are not supposed to participate in domestic politics. When the ambassadors arrived, of course, there were no places for them. All in all, the Democrat's campaign was made to look extremely foolish. It was an event Dick Tuck himself might have been proud of.

FARES
1 RIDE 5¢
G RIDES 25¢
PAY FARE AT TOP

SINAI

DO NOT BOARD A MOVING CAR

STATE SENATOR
TUCK
THE DEMOCRAT

But some of the Nixon campaign's tricks proved to be much dirtier than anything Tuck had ever attempted. These centered on the effort to discredit the campaign of Senator Edmund Muskie, who was for a time the leading candidate for the Democratic nomination for President.

A letter was sent to a newspaper in an important primary state accusing Muskie of using an ethnic slur. Upon investigation, the supposed name and address of the person who sent the letter proved to be false. The letter had apparently been sent by some of Nixon's dirty tricksters. It not only badly embarrassed Muskie but probably cost him many votes from members of the ethnic group involved, as well as from others sensitive to ethnic insults.

Perhaps the worst of all the Segretti tricks involved a letter sent to supporters of a candidate in the Florida Democratic primary, Senator Henry "Scoop" Jackson. It was written on a letterhead stolen from the Muskie campaign by a Segretti spy and purported to come from Muskie's staff.

The letter claimed that Jackson was the father of an illegitimate child and that he had been arrested for homosexual activities. Not content with slandering Jackson, the letter went on to charge that another candidate, Hubert H. Humphrey, had been arrested for drunk driving while in the company of a prostitute.

All of these charges were untrue, but they were cleverly designed to do as much damage as possible to all the Democratic candidates. Voters who believed the charges would be prejudiced against Jackson and Humphrey, while those who saw through the charges would be angered with Muskie for apparently authorizing such a scandalous letter.

Most political observers agree that Segretti's forces went too far. The false accusations of ethnic slurs and immorality

Dick Tuck, the political prankster, ran for state senate in California in 1966.

were clearly unethical and immoral. The courts agreed. Donald Segretti was sentenced to a term in a federal prison for his part in the Florida deception.

But some observers argue that the kinds of dirty tricks practiced by Dick Tuck are another matter. They aren't so much dirty tricks as, they say, harmless pranks. They provide a much-needed touch of humor to a campaign process that is too often not only dull but pompously self-righteous. Even some of Nixon's own campaign people thought Tuck's pranks were funny.

Virtually no one would argue that such tricks are on the same ethical level as Segretti's slanderous campaign letters. Tuck himself was quoted in a *Time* magazine article as making this distinction between his activities and those of Donald Segretti: "I was not surreptitious. I didn't hide what I did. I never tried to be malicious." Yet, despite such differences, many people feel there should be *no* dirty tricks in a political campaign, no matter how amusing they might be. All such tricks interfere, to some degree, with the communication between a candidate and the voting public.

Candidates need the opportunity to communicate their messages to the public, and the public needs to hear them. That is what political campaigns are for. Even at their most high-spirited and unmalicious, dirty tricks disrupt that process. That is their purpose. And it is that purpose, more than the details of any particular trick, which raises the gravest ethical concerns about them.

The Damage Done

The above have been just a few examples of the kinds of unethical tactics that sometimes pollute American political campaigns. It is probably true that most politicians practice only the milder forms of misrepresentation—those that fall under the heading of "polishing their image." No one, after all, wants to proclaim his or her faults to the public in the middle of a political campaign.

Far fewer politicians practice the more drastic forms of deception, such as smearing their opponents and lying to the voters about their true political beliefs and intentions.

But every misrepresentation in a political campaign, like every dirty trick, distorts the process. The voters have to choose someone to represent them in government. To make their best choice, they must know as much as possible, as accurately as possible, about the candidates they must choose between. They have to know who they are and what they stand for. Anything that stands between the voters and that knowledge taints their choice.

Also, although many unethical campaign tactics are minor, they have a cumulative negative effect on our feelings about the electoral process. Public opinion polls continually show that voters distrust the words of politicians. Things have reached a point where many people are not even surprised, much less shocked or offended, when a campaign lie is exposed. Perhaps that is wise, since citizens in a democracy must always be alert to the possibility that their leaders may try to deceive them. But that kind of cynicism can do its own damage. It can dull the ethical sense of politicians and public alike. Most seriously, it tends to undermine our faith in our political system—the faith on which the health of the system ultimately depends.

Stealing
Elections

Vote Fraud

Sometimes unethical practices are carried over from the campaign into the election itself. Over the years, unscrupulous politicians have found many ways to manipulate the voting process. The simplest is buying votes.

It is not known when the first vote was purchased in an American election, but the practice was already established in some places by the 1830s. It was particularly widespread in those areas where the political machines were most powerful. A "machine" is an organization (usually allied to a political party) whose purpose is to control the government of a specific jurisdiction (see chapter 7). In the heyday of the machines, in the nineteenth and the early twentieth centuries, some large cities and even some states were politically dominated by them.

The machines and the practice of buying votes flourished in places where there were large numbers of poor people—people so poor that they would sell their votes cheaply. In some parts of rural America, and in the poor neighborhoods of such cities as New York, Chicago, and Boston, vote buying was blatant. The bosses who ran the party machines would arrive in the neighborhood early on election day, their coat pockets heavy with coins. They would end the day with their pockets empty, the coins all dispensed to eager voters.

The price of a vote varied from place to place and from election to election. In 1832, for example, the Tammany Hall machine in New York City paid five dollars a vote. Only six years later, in 1838, the Whig party paid twenty-two dollars per vote. That was, however, exceptionally high.

While no reliable statistics have been kept, of course, the most commonly quoted price for a vote has typically been five dollars. That's what Tammany Hall paid in 1832 and what the San Antonio, Texas, machine is said to have paid in the 1940s. As late as 1967, it was claimed that the Democratic machine in Albany, New York, was still buying votes at the same price. The consistency of the five dollar figure is deceptive, however. There was a great deal of inflation from 1832 to 1967, and the dollar's value shrank to a fraction of what it had been. This means that the real price of an American vote—illegally purchased, at least— must have actually gone down over the years.

Some industrious voters multiplied their earnings by voting several times. In order to prevent such practices, lists of eligible voters were kept at each polling place. On election day, poll watchers checked voters' names against the names on the list. But this presented no problem for some bosses, who simply paid the poll watchers to look the other way.

At other polls, fraudulent voters would give names that were not their own but were on the voters' list. The machines had registered the names of dead people, taken off the tombstones in the local cemetery. That way, there would not be any embarrassment when the real voters showed up at the polls after someone had already voted in their names.

Perhaps the worst examples of this kind of fraud took place in Philadelphia around the turn of the century. A machine known as the Gas Ring registered not only a number of dead people but several horses and house pets as well.

Such frauds were usually caried off peacefully, but sometimes there was trouble. In 1894, for example, two Republican poll watchers in Troy, New York, tried to interfere with some "repeaters" being "run in" by the Democratic machine. A fight ensued, and before long it turned into a wholesale gun battle between the two factions. By the time the fight was over, two Republicans and one Democrat were dead. The Republicans claimed that the Democrats had started the shooting, while the Democrats blamed the police who were controlled by the Republican city administration. In any case, there wasn't a single arrest, despite the three killings. That level of violence was not common, but election-related violence was far from rare.

It wasn't necessary for every vote—or even a majority of them—to be fraudulent: just enough to push one candidate into a safe lead. In the New York City election of 1868, for example, some 156,000 votes were cast. Of these about 25,000 were later shown to be fraudulent, counting those on both sides. But the majority of contests for city offices were decided by far fewer than 25,000 votes.

In some places, the actual votes didn't matter at all. Dishonest politicians discovered that it could be cheaper to buy off election officials than to buy off voters. There were fewer of them. If the people who counted the votes were "fixed," then it wouldn't matter how many people voted, or how often. They would simply "count" however many votes were needed. In the days when all polling places used paper ballots, it was easy. Even with modern voting machines, it isn't hard. There are ways for dishonest officials to fiddle with voting machines to make them register the desired result.

By all accounts, however, there is much less election

fraud today than there used to be fifty or even thirty years ago. There are several reasons for this apparent decline. Voters are generally better educated than they used to be, and television has helped to make them more politically sophisticated. The most important contributor to the decrease in such practices, however, is probably the decline in the power of the political machines. Still, voting fraud has not been stopped completely. In virtually every national election, charges are made that significant fraud has occurred in some localities.

Stealing a Primary in Texas

Most of the above examples of election fraud took place in large cities. This should not, however, lead you to believe that it is exclusively a big city phenomenon. Small towns and rural districts have also been vulnerable to political misbehavior, and wherever election fraud takes place, its ultimate effects may be felt by the entire country.

A graphic example of this took place in 1948, when a young Democratic congressman from Texas ran for his party's nomination for the U.S. Senate. (Since Texas voters were overwhelmingly Democratic in those days, winning the Democratic primary amounted to winning the Senate seat.) The congressman had the support of a powerful political machine that controlled the votes of a large number of Mexican-Americans in rural south Texas through a combination of bribery and intimidation.

These predominantly poor and uneducated voters were escorted to the polls by armed representatives of the political machine. Some of their escorts carried pistols, some rifles, and some both. The voters were given either money or tequila in return for their votes, and their gun-carrying guards watched to make sure they voted the way they were told. This practice was common in that part of Texas at the time.

Despite this "support" from the machine, the election

returns showed that the congressman had lost the nomination by 112 votes statewide. The local machine immediately "found" 201 more votes for the congressman—votes the machine's own officials had somehow "overlooked" in the first count. Despite the fact that everyone with any knowledge of Texas politics was convinced that the 201 votes were fraudulent, the congressman was declared the Democratic nominee, and as such he easily won election to the Senate.

Although his victory seemed to be strictly a Texas affair, it proved to have national significance. The congressman, who had previously been all but unknown nationally, used his seat in the Senate to gain national prominence. Senator Lyndon Johnson rapidly became the majority leader of the U.S. Senate, from which post he went on to become vice president of the United States under John F. Kennedy, and ultimately President.

It is not clear how deeply, if at all, Johnson was involved in the unethical activities the machine conducted on his behalf. It is quite possible that he was never actually informed of the methods being used to extort votes for him. But Johnson was already a skilled and experienced Texas politician, and he must have known what kinds of tactics his supporters customarily employed. Nonetheless, he gladly accepted both their support and the 201 votes they so mysteriously "discovered" after the fact. However deeply he was personally involved, it seems clear that without seemingly local election fraud in Texas, he might never have become a national political figure, much less President of the United States.

Stealing the Presidency

Some historians believe that the presidency itself has been "stolen" by unethical tactics—and on more than one occasion. They believe that certain presidential elections would have had different results had it not been for some form of political corruption, and that different men would have been elected President.

One such disputed election took place in 1824. It was seriously complicated by the electoral college. The "college" is made up of electors chosen by the individual states. The number of electors from each state is determined by the number of senators and representatives from each state. The electors meet following the general election, and it is they who officially elect the President of the United States by a majority vote. Constitutionally, some experts have argued that they are free to vote for any candidate they choose to be President, regardless of whom the electorate thought it was voting for. In practice, however, they are expected to reflect the will of the voters of their state.

The Constitution originally left it up to the state governments to determine who would represent them in the electoral college in any way they chose. If no candidate got a majority of the electoral votes, the choice of a President would be turned over to the U.S. House of Representatives. By 1824, a majority of the states—eighteen out of twenty-four—had decided to choose their electors by popular vote, which means the direct vote of the eligible voters of the state. The voters voted for electors pledged to specific candidates. For the first time, the President would be determined primarily, although indirectly, by popular vote.

Electors pledged to Andrew Jackson received more popular votes than those pledged to any other candidate. Jackson had 99 electoral votes, compared to 84 for the second-place candidate, John Quincy Adams—although Adams had actually carried more states than Jackson. There were several candidates, however, and Jackson's 99 votes did not constitute a majority.

When the decision was thrown to the House, the votes of the people were largely ignored. Political deals resulted in the House giving the presidency to Adams, who had received not only fewer popular votes but also fewer electoral votes than Jackson.

Although many citizens resented this action, the House had the constitutional authority to act as it did. The result was undemocratic, in the sense that the candidate who had received the greatest number of popular votes was passed over for one who had received fewer votes. But, because of the procedure established by the Constitution, the result had been achieved legally. The ethics of the House action were arguable, however.

Fifty-two years later came what many believe to have been the most blatantly unethical presidential election in American history. In 1876, the Civil War hero Ulysses S. Grant was stepping down as President, and the question was, who would succeed him?

Ironically, considering how the election campaign would be conducted, both parties nominated political reformers. Grant's Republicans put up Rutherford B. Hayes, the governor of Ohio. The Democrats nominated the governor of New York, Samuel J. Tilden, who had made a popular reputation for himself attacking corrupt political machines.

A great issue was at stake in the election: the future of Reconstruction in the South. Hayes, and the Republicans generally, favored the continuation of the harsh Reconstructionist policies that had been put in effect to secure the civil and political rights of the recently freed black slaves. Tilden and the Democrats opposed most of those measures. They believed that Reconstruction was designed to punish the South and that the time had come to heal the wounds of the Civil War, not to rub salt in them.

Rutherford B. Hayes, the Republican presidential candidate in 1876, went on to become the nineteenth president.

The election campaign was extraordinarily bitter. Forces on both sides, with or without the knowledge of the candidates, used a variety of illegal and sometimes vicious measures to ensure their victory. The Republicans, who had the power of the federal government at their command, since Grant was still President, used armed troops in several of the southern states, not just to protect Hayes voters but to intimidate Tilden voters as well.

On the other side, the Ku Klux Klan, allied to the local Democrats, used every means it could—including cold-blooded murder—to keep black voters away from the polls.

When the votes were counted, Tilden seemed to have won the election. Of the electoral votes not in dispute, Tilden had 184, while Hayes had only 163. But 184 was one short of the majority necessary to make Tilden President.

The 19 electoral votes of three southern states— Louisiana, South Carolina, and Florida—remained officially uncounted because of charges of election irregularities. (Three other electoral votes, in Oregon, were also in dispute.) These were the three states in which fraud, violence, and intimidation had been most rampant, and neither side would acknowledge defeat. Each state had two election boards, one Democratic and the other Republican. The Democratic board in each state claimed that its count proved that Tilden had won while the Republican boards all claimed that Hayes was the winner. Logic seemed to favor the Democrats, since the 19 votes were all in southern states where Democratic sympathy was strong among white voters.

Although various elements of Reconstruction, including the presence of federal troops, complicated matters, it seemed virtually certain that Tilden would pick up the

Samuel J. Tilden, the Democratic
candidate for president in 1876

single electoral vote he needed to claim the presidency. The Congress, however, formed a special election commission to decide the issue. It was made up of seven Republicans, seven Democrats, and one member without party affiliation who was later replaced by an eighth Republican.

Many historians agree that if the commission had acted impartially, attempting simply to decide whom the people had chosen, Tilden would have become President. Instead, Congress and the commission seem to have cut a political deal. The Republican, Hayes, would become President, despite the fact that Tilden had received over 250,000 more popular votes. In return for the Democratic Congress's acceptance of this decision, the Republicans agreed to pull the federal troops out of the southern states. In essence, the Republicans and Democrats had made a trade: the presidency for an end to Reconstruction.

Congress could argue that the trade had been ethical. They were empowered to make a deal by the Constitution, and, as politicians, their business was compromise. All they had done was to forge a compromise between the interests of two sections of the country.

On the other hand, it can be argued that they would not have been in a position to make such a compromise—and to overrule the decision of the voters—had it not been for the rampantly unethical practices of both parties in the election.

In any case, the longest lasting result of the election of 1876 was the end of Reconstruction, which meant the end of any serious effort to protect the rights of black people in the United States for nearly a century to come.

The elections of 1824 and 1876 were not the only presidential elections in which election fraud was claimed. One of the most dramatic was that of 1960, in which John F. Kennedy and his running mate Lyndon Johnson narrowly defeated Richard Nixon and Henry Cabot Lodge. The popular vote was extremely close, with Kennedy winning by about 115,000 out of almost 69 million votes. It was especially close in two big electoral states, Illinois and Texas, both of which went to Kennedy and both of which had long histories of corruption. Nixon's supporters charged that fraudulent votes in Chicago—whose Democratic boss, Mayor Richard J. Daley, was an ally of Kennedy—and in rural Texas, where the machine was allied to Johnson, had thrown the states to the Democrats. If Illinois and Texas had gone to Nixon, he would have won the election.

4

The Importance of Money

If elections are the heart's blood of our political system, money is the heart's blood of our elections. It costs money to win elections to public office in this country. It even costs money to *lose*. In general, the higher the office and the larger the constituency, the more it is likely to cost, win or lose.

It was not always so expensive. In the first presidential "campaign," George Washington, who ran unopposed, spent nothing at all. By the mid-nineteenth century, however, elections were already becoming expensive. The Republicans spent at least $100,000 to elect Abraham Lincoln in 1860, and forty years later the same party managed to spend $6 million in behalf of William McKinley. Even allowing for the fact that the McKinley forces were unusually spendthrift, money was clearly beginning to play an important part in national political campaigns.

In this century, campaign costs have soared. In 1984, for

example, the Republicans reported spending $42,560,761.71 to re-elect President Ronald Reagan and Vice President George Bush. In the same election the Democrats reported spending $43,027,413.72 in behalf of the losing candidates, Walter Mondale and Geraldine Ferraro.

There are several reasons for these enormous costs. The first is simply that the electorate—the voters whom candidates have to reach—has gotten bigger. There are more than seven times as many people in the United States today as there were in Lincoln's time. The second reason is that this voting population is spread out over a huge geographical area, from Florida to Alaska and from Maine to Hawaii. What is more, this large and far-flung electorate is more politically independent than it used to be.

At one time, the majority of voters were either loyal Republicans or loyal Democrats, who voted dependably for all the candidates of their party. Today, many make a habit of "splitting their ballots"—voting for Democrats for some offices, Republicans for others, and independents or candidates of minor parties for others still. This new independence means that candidates have to campaign more extensively than before. Voters who could once be counted on now have to be persuaded. And that takes money. Lots of money.

The mass media take much of that money, and television takes most of that. Major national campaigns in recent years have been conducted largely on television, and television time is expensive. In 1984, for example, the Television Bureau of Advertising determined that the *average* cost for thirty seconds of prime time on a national television network was $107, 500!

Television is not the only technical innovation in modern politics. New polling techniques, the direct mailing of campaign literature, and other new campaigning methods have revolutionized the way campaigns are conducted. All of these—along with the armies of consultants, makeup experts, speech writers, and other specialists hired to help out in campaigns today—add to the costs of a modern campaign.

On the federal level alone, candidates for the House and Senate spent a reported $374.6 million in 1984. (And these are just the *reported* expenses. It is virtually certain that millions more went unreported for a variety of reasons.) Add to this the more than $85 million reportedly spent on the presidential and vice presidential races, plus the many millions spent on the thousands upon thousands of local, county, and state elections that year, and it is likely that political campaigning is a billion dollar business in the United States today!

This need for money puts serious ethical pressures on our politicians. Some observers, including many politicians themselves, believe that the pressure for money is becoming so great that it threatens the integrity of the entire political process. To understand the full significance and depth of this perceived threat, it is necessary to understand not only the enormous need for money in the modern campaign process, but also to understand something about where that money comes from, who contributes it, how, and why.

Big Business

Over the almost two hundred years of American political campaigning, there have been dramatic changes in the way campaigns are paid for. At first, campaign financing presented little or no ethical problem. Most candidates paid for their own campaigns. When expenses got too high, friends would chip in to help.

By the mid-19th century, however, campaigns had become so expensive that only the wealthiest politicians could afford to pay for them out of their own pockets. Most needed outside sources of funds. One place they found them was in newly established organizations called political parties. These organizations, made up of people with common political interests, pooled the resources of their members to help finance candidates who shared those interests.

Others, both individuals and organizations, also contributed to campaigns. Many of these were ordinary citizens —farmers, small-business people, skilled laborers, and the like—who contributed small amounts. But some were far from ordinary. They were individuals of great wealth, or powerful corporations. They were different from most contributors because they could afford to contribute large sums of money to the candidates they supported.

Something else set many of these large contributors apart. They were not contributing merely because they admired a specific candidate or agreed with his views. They had specific objectives in mind. There were things they wanted from the government—things like public lands to use for their own profit, tax advantages, and laws that would make it hard for their employees to form labor unions. Some of these contributors were interested not in the public good but in their own private needs. They were concerned not with what the politicians would do for the country but with what the politicians would do for *them*. Because their concerns were so narrow and specific, they came to be known as the special interests.

For much of the nineteenth and the early twentieth centuries, most special interests were primarily concerned with economic matters. The most pervasive of them were the big businesses—railroads, mining, oil, manufacturing, and the trusts. However, these were not the only special interests even then. There were the large agricultural interests, for example, including the southern cotton growers, and at least one special interest whose goals were not economic at all. This was the Abolitionist movement, which campaigned against slavery in the years leading up to the Civil War. But aside from the Abolitionists, it was the big business interests that would have the greatest impact on American politics, and would have its impact for the longest time.

Big businesses were in a position to pay for what they wanted from government, and that is precisely what they did. They financed candidates who would work to further

the interests of the business community over those of the labor and consumer sectors of the economy. They made sure that these candidates had more than enough money to get elected.

The relationship between the big businesses and the candidates they supported was quite clear at that time. It was spelled out by the Republican political boss of Pennsylvania (and U.S. senator), Boies Penrose. "You send us to Congress," he told business leaders, and "we pass the laws under . . . which you make money. . . . Out of your profits you further contribute to our campaign funds to send us back again to pass more laws to enable you to make more money."

Penrose certainly kept his part of the bargain. In his twenty-five years in the Senate, he virtually controlled the finance committee, using his position to support high tariffs on foreign products coming into the United States. Those tariffs protected the big businesses, allowing them to set their prices to American customers without fear of foreign competition. The businesses they protected, of course, were primarily the ones that had sent Penrose to Congress. The businesses kept their part of the bargain, too. Penrose was supplied with enough campaign funds to keep him in Congress until he died in 1921.

Some politicians defended these kinds of relationships, arguing that, as President Calvin Coolidge put it, "The business of America is business," and that what was good for business was good for the country. Others felt that the political power of the business interests effectively prevented other Americans from receiving their proper representation in government. Certainly Congress passed a great deal of legislation supported by big business from the time of the Civil War until well into the twentieth century, and very little that was opposed to it.

The relationship between the big business special interests and the politicians they support is more complicated and less clear cut today. Voters have become more wary of politicians' ties to special interests in general, and politicians have become less open about them. Few, if any, would have the courage to spell things out the way Boies Penrose did. But candidates need more money today than ever, and big businesses continue to contribute large amounts, directly and indirectly, to political campaigns.

They are not the only ones.

Other Special Interests

Despite the efforts of the big businesses and their friends in government to prevent it, unions had managed to organize many American industries by the middle of the twentieth century. As the number of union members grew, so did the unions' treasuries. Some unions used part of this money to support political candidates.

Their purpose was clear. Politicians supported by big business had dominated economic and social policy for decades. The unions believed that they also needed a voice in government, and that meant electing politicians sympathetic to them. The way American politics had developed— thanks largely to big business and its campaign-financing practices—that meant supplying friendly candidates with money. But money was not the only thing the unions had to offer a political candidate. They had people. They could supply two things business couldn't: the votes of their members, and volunteers to work in the campaign.

This was an important development in the history of American politics. Big labor, as it came to be known, had become a special interest itself. By midcentury, it would become an extremely powerful one, although not yet as powerful as big business.

Other special interests also began to increase their political influence. Many of these were membership organizations that used their influence to promote the economic, social, and political interests of their members. Each did what it could to persuade or pressure politicians (which is to say, the government) to act on its behalf.

"Lobbies don't kill legislation;
People kill legislation."

Among those that still have a major impact on American politics today are such groups as the American Medical Association, made up of medical doctors; the National Education Association, made up mostly of teachers; and the National Rifle Association, made up mostly of gun owners. Like the unions, many of these organizations have used their large memberships as an effective political weapon.

By now there are few Americans left who are not represented by at least one special interest group. There are organizations representing consumers, small-business people, nurses, snowmobile riders, parents, independent contractors, nudists, pet owners, and almost every other social, economic, and political division imaginable. Many of these are small and relatively insignificant politically. Others have demonstrated their power by playing important, even deciding roles in important elections. Several have firmly established themselves as powerful forces in American political life.

Some observers see those forces as ominous threats to our political system. They believe that the power of the special interests works against the general interest. To the extent that politicians are persuaded to favor a special interest, these observers argue, they must turn their backs on the interests of the rest of society. If business is given a tax break, other taxpayers will have to pay more. If nurses are allowed to strike, patients will suffer. And so on.

Others see no conflict between the special interests and the general interest. Each special interest, they argue, actually represents a portion of the general interest. Just as the three branches of government—the legislative, executive, and judicial—act as checks and balances on one another, the various special interests will balance one another out. If business pressures for a tax break for itself, ordinary taxpayers will pressure for tax breaks of their own. If nurses pressure for the right to strike, patients will pressure against it.

Critics respond that the checks and balances in our governmental structure are planned. The power of each

"I'M NOBODY'S PUPPET!"

[*Former Environmental Protection Agency
director Anne Burford—depicted here
as Miss Piggy—was accused by critics
of being a puppet of special interests.*]

branch of government is defined and limited by law. This is not true of the special interests. Some are much more powerful than others. Each will try to become as powerful and to put as much pressure on our politicians as it can. And more and more they will exercise that power through the use of money.

As we have seen, money is vital to the American election process as it exists today. As campaign costs have soared, the contributions of some of the special interest groups have provided an increasingly significant portion of total campaign financing. In this way, they have made themselves into an indispensable element of the campaign-financing process.

This enormous power was certainly never foreseen, much less intended, by the framers of the Constitution. That document was drawn up at a time when money was an insignificant factor in American elections. This fact has led many thoughtful Americans to ask the question: Is this power—the power of money—whether wielded by wealthy individuals or by special interest groups, a corrupting influence in American political life? Does it have the effect of turning our politicians away from their duty to serve the interests of the public as a whole? Does it lead them to concentrate their efforts on serving the special interests of certain wealthy and powerful groups at the expense of the rest of the citizenry?

Former U.S. Senator Richard S. Schweiker, of Pennsylvania, sorts through seven hundred letters received from coal miners and widows from northeast Pennsylvania asking for help in getting federal benefits for victims of black lung, a terrible disease affecting coal miners.

Ethical Pressures

The Secret Contributors

What do those who contribute heavily to political parties and candidates expect to get for their money?

Different contributors, of course, expect different things. In general, however, contributors can be divided into two broad categories. The first consists of those who are plainly dishonest, whose contributions are usually made in secret, and whose purposes are hidden from public view.

In the past, large contributions might have been kept secret out of an innocent desire on the part of the contributor to remain anonymous. Today, however, there are laws requiring that the identities of large contributors to federal election campaigns be revealed. They make it reasonable to assume that any large contribution made secretly today has a corrupt purpose, if only because it is illegal to make such a contribution.

Some unethical contributors want to buy specific favors with their money. Others want to buy the politicians, and the power of their public offices, outright. These look at the money as a kind of retainer, a fee to make sure that the politician's services will be available whenever they are required.

In the nineteenth century, for example, when the railroads were busy tying the nation together with bands of iron, they needed the cooperation of many state governments. They got it, along with the services of many state politicians, by the lavish expenditure of money. It was widely acknowledged in those days that the big railroads "owned" the entire legislatures of some states. They could call on them whenever they wanted to, and they often did.

A more recent example was that of the eccentric businessman Howard Hughes, who in 1968 contributed heavily —and secretly—to the presidential campaigns of both the Republican Richard Nixon and the Democrat Hubert Humphrey. On the evidence of recently published memos, there is no question that Hughes's purpose was corrupt. He was attempting to buy not just two politicians, but the office of President itself. Since he did not know who would win the election, he tried to make sure he achieved his goal by contributing heavily to both candidates. It is not known how Nixon and Humphrey regarded the money they got from Hughes. All that is known for sure is that they, or high officials in their campaigns, accepted the secret money.

The fact that contributors may have an unethical purpose does not mean that they will get what they pay for. After the 1968 contributions from Hughes, for example, Nixon won the election, but Hughes was often disappointed in his investment. The businessman made several requests for presidential favors, some of which were only partially granted and some of which were turned down flat.

The attitude of some politicians toward such secret money is revealed by the following story told about the flamboyant Huey Long by one of his relatives. A cement contractor gave a large amount of money to Long's successful campaign for governor of Louisiana in 1928. Shortly after the election, the contractor went to Long's office to see him. The man was obviously angry, and the governor's secretary told him Long was too busy to talk that day. The contractor came back the next day, only to be told the same thing. He returned again the following day. And the next.

Finally, the enraged contractor insisted he be allowed to see the governor. The secretary said she'd see what she could do and went into Long's office. "That contractor's back again," she told him. "And he's all upset."

"Oh," asked Long innocently, "why is that?"

"Well," the secretary responded, "he says you promised him that if he contributed to your campaign, you'd give him the contract to build the new state highway. Well, he gave you the money, and now he hears you've given the contract to somebody else. He says he's not leaving here until he gets an explanation. What should I tell him?"

Long grinned. "Tell him I lied," he said.

The story raises an interesting ethical question. The initial bribe was clearly both illegal and unethical. But, having accepted it, would it have been more ethical for Long to honor his unethical commitment to the cement contractor and give him the promised contract? Or was it more ethical for him to do as he did? A similar situation once prompted a disappointed political boss to define an honest politician as "one who stays bought."

The Open Contributors— Buying Access

Most large contributors today do not fall into the category discussed above. They are both less ambitious than the nineteenth-century railroad owners and more sophisticated than the Louisiana cement contractor. They don't offer crude bribes, and they don't try to buy politicians outright. They report their contributions and other expenditures as the law requires them to do. They don't intend to do anything illegal, just to "play the political game" according to the rules set down by the state and federal legislatures.

Nevertheless, they, too, must expect something in return for their money or they wouldn't give it.

Politicians often rail against the special interests, particularly those special interests that contribute to their opponents' campaigns. These politicians suggest that *other* politicians are somehow unfairly influenced by those contributions. But if you ask the same politicians what it is that their own financial supporters get for their money, they will deny that they get anything.

Many large contributors say much the same thing. They say that they support candidates because they believe in them, agree with their political views, and feel confident that they will do a good job in office—*not* because they expect any favors in return.

Ask other contributors and politicians, however, and they will admit that most large contributors *do* expect something in return for their money. At the very least, they expect access. And they get it.

In political terms, access means the right to speak to public officials, to have them listen to you and take your views into account. For the special interests, access is an extremely valuable asset, and one way to ensure it is to be an important financial supporter of a candidate or political party.

The question can be asked: What is wrong with the special interests (or anyone else) getting access to public officials by donating to their campaigns? As we have seen, campaigns cost money, and the money has to come from somewhere. Why shouldn't a contributor be listened to and taken seriously? The special interests are not a foreign, hostile force attacking the American political system. They represent the needs and views of large numbers of American citizens. Shouldn't they be heard? For that matter, shouldn't all citizens be heard? Ideally, shouldn't *everyone* have access?

Whatever the ideal, the reality is that public officials are usually very busy people with great demands on their

"INSTEAD OF RELYING ON ME, WHY DON'T YOU JUST
PULL YOURSELF UP BY THE BOOTSTRAPS?"

time. They deal with issues of great importance to all levels of society. They make decisions that affect everyone's health, economic well-being, and, ultimately, survival. It is inevitable that many people want to talk to them—to explain their problems to them, to ask for their help, and to persuade them to act in their behalf. But few citizens have the opportunity to do more than shake politicians' hands at political rallies or write them letters that may or may not be read.

There might be tens of thousands of small contributors to a U.S. senator's re-election campaign, and only a handful of organizations and individuals who contribute large amounts. But a senator does not have the time to sit down and talk with tens of thousands of people. The reality is that he or she will only be able to talk to a relatively small number of constituents. And, the need for money being as great as it is, it is virtually certain that the large contributors will have first claim on the senator's time and attention.

What is more, the line between access and influence is very thin, particularly when large sums of money have been spent and the politician knows that large sums of money are going to be needed again for the next election.

Is this advantage granted the large contributor ethical? Is it proper that certain citizens should have a greater opportunity than others to influence their elected officials? Public officials, after all, have a duty to serve all citizens, not just those wealthy enough or organized enough to contribute substantial amounts to political campaigns. Should money be an important, even a determining factor in deciding who gets access to public officials? Whether it should be or not, it is generally acknowledged that it is.

The PACs

In the past, large contributors were usually wealthy individuals or corporations. Recently, however, important changes have been made in the way the special interests finance political campaigns. Because of certain changes in the law, most now make their political contributions through institutions called political action committees, or PACs.

The PACs have grown so large that some politicians believe they allow the special interests to exert destructive power over the American political system. Ironically, they originally came about as an indirect result of an attempt to *curb* the political power of a special interest.

In the 1940s, labor unions were forbidden to use their treasuries to make political contributions. The reason was that union treasuries were made up of dues collected from union members, and such contributions forced the individual members to support political candidates chosen by the union, whether the members approved of them or not. This was considered unfair. Later on, corporations were forbidden to use corporate operating funds to make political contributions for much the same reason.

Searching for a way to get around this prohibition, the unions hit on the idea of establishing committees to handle their political contributions. These committees would not use union treasury funds. Instead, they would appeal to the membership for voluntary contributions. The PACs proved to be both legal and effective as a means of distributing money for political purposes. They allowed the unions not only to maintain but to increase their influence during the next few decades.

In the wake of the Watergate scandal (see Chapter 7), Congress passed legislation limiting the amount of money any contributor, including a PAC, could contribute to any candidate's campaign to $1,000. At first this seemed to be a serious blow to the political power of big money, whether it came from business or labor or anywhere else. The PACs, however, soon found ways to get around these new regulations and to keep their power.

A loophole in the law allowed most PACs to qualify for a much higher contribution limit. And even after that

limit had been reached, the PACs discovered that they could expend virtually unlimited amounts of money so long as it was not in the form of a direct contribution to a specific candidate or campaign.

But perhaps the most direct way the special interest groups discovered to get around the contribution limit was to form more PACs. By the mid-1970s, there were more than 200 labor-sponsored PACs. But they were no longer alone.

Other special interests had learned from the unions and started their own PACs. While the unions had their 200-plus PACs by 1974, business corporations already had some 89 of their own. More than 300 PACs had also been formed by other special interest groups, each having its own impact on the political process.

PACs can be divided into five categories: the labor PACs, sponsored by unions; corporate PACs, sponsored by businesses; trade, membership, and health PACs; nonconnected PACs, many of which promote political ideologies; and a general category of other PACs that don't fit into any of the first four categories.

Over the past decade, the number of PACs in each category has grown dramatically. But the number of labor PACs has grown the least. The number of corporate PACs, on the other hand, has grown the most. In the six years from 1975 to 1981, for example, the number of PACs sponsored by labor grew from 226 to 318. In the same period, the number of corporate PACs leaped from 139 to 1,327. Today, there are over 4,000 PACs, all of them doing their best to exert pressure on the American political system, to bend it to their will.

Their financial resources give the PACs enormous political influence. They are often the largest contributors to particular campaigns, and it is primarily through them that the special interests filter their money, and their influence, into the American political system. Their financial power was clearly demonstrated in the 1984 elections. PACs of all kinds raised approximately $295.4 million for those elections, of which they actually spent some $273.2 million. That is more than half of all the money spent by the candidates and the two major political parties combined.

The most dramatic increase in the number and power of the PACs has come in the category of nonconnected, or ideological, PACs. The most effective of these has probably been the National Conservative Political Action Committee (or NCPAC), which supports conservative causes and candidates. In an effort to fight the financial restrictions placed on the PACs, NCPAC recently went before the Supreme Court and won a case that authorized unlimited spending by independent PACs and individuals—that is, by those not formally connected to political parties or candidates. As a result, such spending will be more important than ever in future elections.

Already in the 1984 elections, the spending by such independents added up to more than $23 million, the great bulk of it spent in behalf of conservative candidates. Some $15.8 million went to support Ronald Reagan's candidacy, for example, while only $803,923 was spent in behalf of Walter Mondale's. The largest of the independent PAC contributors was NCPAC itself, which spent $9.8 million in Reagan's behalf, $289, 995 *against* Mondale, and $116,000 more *against* thirteen liberal Democrats and one moderate Republican running for other federal offices.

By contrast, the largest individual spender in the 1984 campaign was a real estate developer from California who reported spending $419,573 to defeat a liberal Republican senator from Illinois. Whatever the true amount, it seems clear that the expenditures of even the largest individual contributors are being dwarfed by those of the largest PACs.

The combined economic power of the PACs creates a heavy financial pressure not only on many politicians, but on the political system itself. And in politics, financial pressure often means ethical pressure as well. There is an old saying that "he who pays the piper calls the tune."

Few politicians would argue that there is anything inherently unethical about a political contribution as such. Money can be contributed to political campaigns without either the intention or the effect of corrupting the candidate. This is generally agreed to be true of the small, anonymous contributions of five to ten dollars that are made by most individual contributors. Citizens in a democracy, after all, have every right to support candidates with whom they agree. They may even have an ethical duty to do so. With a small contribution, particularly one given anonymously, there is not likely to be any intent to corrupt. Even if there were, it seems unlikely that any politician would be tempted to betray the public trust for such a small amount of money.

When it comes to larger contributions or other expenditures on a candidate's behalf, however, some observers see a greater ethical danger. Many of them, including several politicians, believe things have reached a real danger point with the PACs. They believe that the economic power of these committees has become so great that it threatens the ethical integrity of the entire political system.

Other politicians disagree. They say there is no real ethical difference between a large campaign contribution and a small one. They accept PAC support cheerfully and argue that they are in no way corrupted by it.

But critics of the PACs do not argue that PAC contributions are necessarily intended as bribes, nor do they contend that every politician who accepts help from a PAC is corrupt. They acknowledge that most politicians do their best to act ethically and honestly and to live up to their public trust.

The true ethical danger, as they see it, is not that the PACs corrupt individual politicians by causing them to act unethically. The danger is that the enormous financial power of the PACs taken together corrupts the political system itself. It distorts it. PAC money, they say, has the effect of unbalancing the political process, tilting it dangerously away from the rights of ordinary citizens and toward the special interests.

The PACs funnel most of their money into House and Senate campaigns. For this reason, senators and members of the House of Representatives are probably the most sensitive of all politicians to the pressures exerted by the economic power of the PACs. Many of them are made extremely uncomfortable by those pressures. Some have tried to do something about them.

In 1983, a group of congressmen, headed by Wisconsin Democrat Dave Obey who has led the House on this issue, offered legislation to limit the power of the PACs. "The pressure generated by [the PACs] is enormous," the congressmen announced, "and it warps the process." They went on to describe the effects of that pressure in a telling phrase. "It creates," they said, "the politics of intimidation."

Those are powerful words—"the politics of intimidation." But what did the congressmen mean by them? How do the voluntary contributions of the PACs, voluntarily accepted, intimidate members of the U.S. Congress?

It is done, say the congressmen, with the "carrots and sticks of campaign money." The phrase comes from rabbit hunting. It refers to a two-way effort to flush a rabbit out of the bushes. A carrot is used to tempt it out from the front, while a stick is used to chase it out from behind.

The carrot the special interests use is obvious—large expenditures made in behalf of friendly politicians. The stick is the threat that even larger expenditures might be made for the politician's opponent if the politician won't cooperate. That threat is rarely, if ever, stated. But, say the congressmen, it is always there.

The pressure, like the threat, is often subtle. It is not that many representatives and senators make a conscious decision to violate their personal beliefs and the interests of their constituents in order to please a PAC. It is more that the presence of the big-money PACs, with the financial resources they control, creates a new and ethically more dangerous context in which Congress has to conduct the nation's business. Both the carrot and the stick are realities the senators and House members have to take into account, whether they succumb to them or not. It is impossible to say to what extent individual politicians are swayed by those realities. The truth about that rests inside their minds and consciences. But the group of congressmen led by David Obey believe , as do others, that Congress as a whole is vulnerable to the pressure from the PACs.

As they see it, the PACs mean that "Washington-based lobbies can squeeze and dominate Congress," overriding the interests of those citizens not represented by a large and wealthy PAC. If they are right, the reality of PAC influence runs contrary to the principles stated in the Preamble to the Constitution, which calls for a government that will "promote the general welfare." As things stand, at least where Congress is concerned, the interests of the public at large may be less important than the special interests represented by the PACs.

Although many politicians resent this intimidation by the PACs, Congress has proven unable to effectively curtail their power. The members of the House have to face re-election every two years, which creates a nearly constant need for campaign funds. Many representatives are reluctant to shut off a major source of such funds. (That fact, in itself, shows the power of the PACs to intimidate Congress.) Although some, like Obey and his colleagues, are willing to take that risk, it seems that most are not. The outlook for effective reform, reform that would destroy the PACs' key role in financing election campaigns, is dim.

Conflicts
of Interest

Private Interests

Conflicts of interest occur when a public official's duties come into conflict with his or her private interests. The term "interest," in this sense, does not refer to curiosity. Rather, it means a personal share or stake in something. When speaking of political conflicts of interest, the term "private interest" usually implies an *economic* interest— that is, something from which the official stands to benefit financially. The mere existence of a conflict of interest raises an ethical question: Can public officials fairly represent both the public interest and their own?

There are various kinds and degrees of conflict of interest. Some examples might be a senator who owns stock in a bank but who sits on a committee that writes laws to regulate banks; a federal official who awards defense contracts to electronics firms and who has an arrangement to work for them as a consultant after leaving the government; a member of Congress who owns a farm and sponsors a bill exempting farmers from certain taxes. In all these cases, the officials are in a position to take action as public servants that could affect their private financial well-being. All these situations raise serious ethical concerns for the officials involved.

Some critics would argue that *any* conflict of interest is inherently unethical. The political columnist Walter Lippmann, for example, once used conflict of interest as the very definition of political corruption: "The grafter," he maintained, "is a man whose loyalty is divided and whose motives are mixed . . . a public official who serves a private interest. . . . The attempt to serve at the same time two antagonistic interests is what constitutes corruption."

Extreme critics like Lippmann would argue that any official facing even the slightest conflict of interest must withdraw from it. The official must either eliminate the source of the conflict or remove himself or herself from any action involving it. The bank-owning senator, for example, must either sell the stock in the bank or step down from the committee that regulates banks. The federal official must either quit the government job or give up the ambition to work for the electronics firms in the future. The farm-owning member of Congress must either sell the farm or refuse to sponsor, or even vote on, farm tax legislation.

Few politicians would hold to a standard as strict as that. While recognizing the real ethical problems involved, most would argue that some conflict of interest has to be tolerated, if only because it is inevitable. Consider the question of income tax laws, for example. Such laws affect everyone who receives any significant amount of income. Members of the House and Senate receive congressional salaries and are therefore affected by the income tax laws. But they have a duty to vote on all new income tax legislation. If all conflicts of interest had to be scrupulously avoided, the Congress would never be able to act on an income tax bill.

Along with such inevitable conflicts of interest, there are others that are all but unavoidable. Most people elected

"MY OUTSIDE INCOME IS FROM
SPEECHES, MAGAZINE ARTICLES,
AND A CONFLICT OF INTEREST
INVOLVING A CHEMICAL PLANT."

to the Senate in recent years have been lawyers, and yet laws have to be passed relating to the legal profession. The majority of the members of state legislatures around the country are either married or divorced, yet laws have to be passed relating to marriage and divorce. And so on.

It seems unrealistic, then, to expect public officials to avoid all conflicts of interest.

The Public Interest

Some conflicts of interest may even be desirable. At least, many voters seem to think so. It is common for people who work in or own oil-related businesses to be elected to the state legislatures in oil-producing states, for example. Nor is it unusual for someone in agriculture to be elected in a farm state.

Analysis suggests that many people who voted for these candidates did so not in spite of their business interests but because of them. The voters, too, had a private interest in those industries, and they wanted someone in office who shared that interest. They wanted someone who would, in promoting his or her own interest, promote theirs as well.

It can even be argued that this kind of conflict of interest is a positive good. If that is what the voters want, that is what they should get. Senator Robert Kerr of Oklahoma once argued exactly that. "I represent the financial institutions of Oklahoma," he acknowledged. "I am interested in them, and that is the reason they elect me. They wouldn't want to send a man here [to the Senate] who has no community of interest with them, because he wouldn't be worth a nickel to them."

On the other hand, it can be argued that even a widely shared private interest is not the same thing as the public interest. At the same time, the fact that a private interest is shared by many voters does not remove the ethical duty of a politician to act in the public interest.

Take the case of a hypothetical state legislator named Mary, who comes from a district in which a chemical company is the principal employer. The company wants the legislature to pass a special law permitting it to dump a toxic chemical into an important state river. It claims that if it does not get the permission, it will lose a great deal of money, its stockholders will suffer, and many workers will be laid off. Because the majority of people in Mary's district either work for the company or have relatives who do, the company asks Mary to sponsor the bill.

As the situation has been stated so far, there seems to be no problem for Mary. The voters of Mary's district all share an economic interest in this particular chemical company. But is that common interest a public interest? It may or may not be, depending not only on how "public interest" is defined but also on how the interest of voters in Mary's district may affect the interests of other members of the public who do not live in that district and do not have a direct tie to the chemical company.

Suppose that a number of scientific experts, hired by the state, inform Mary that dumping the chemical would have disastrous effects on the ecology of the river as well as on the economic and physical health of people all over the state. They explain that the chemical would kill all the fish in the river, thus destroying a large fishing industry downriver from the chemical plant, and out of Mary's district. That would mean far more people would lose their jobs in the fishing industry than would lose their jobs at the chemical company if it were forbidden to dump.

Suppose further that the state's scientists testify that the chemical is likely to get into the groundwater, contaminating the drinking water of thousands of people, making them sick or even killing them. It could, in effect, make a large area of the state virtually uninhabitable for decades to come.

Clearly, while many people in Mary's district have an interest in the chemical company getting permission to dump, that permission would not be in the interest of many other people in the rest of the state. Can it then be truly in the public interest? If Mary desires to act ethically, that is something she will have to decide.

She must weigh at least two equations. First, she must balance the economic interests of the people of her district, who would benefit, against the economic interests of the people elsewhere in the state, who would be hurt. In the example cited, more people would be injured economically if the chemical were dumped than would be helped. On that ground, Mary might well decide to refuse to sponsor the bill. On the other hand, she might decide that her first duty is to promote the interest of the people in her own district, and therefore she might decide to go ahead and sponsor the bill.

The second equation has to do with the kinds and degrees of benefits or harm that might result from her action. In this case, the interests that will be helped if the company gets the permission are economic. The company will not lose money, and Mary's constituents will not lose jobs. On the other side of the equation, the interests that will be hurt are only partly economic. People in the fishing industry will lose their jobs, and many people may become sick or even die because of the polluted groundwater. Mary, then, must weigh the health interests of some citizens of the state against the economic interests of the voters of her district.

You might ask yourself how you would decide if you were Mary. Which of these interests most truly represents the *public* interest? Should Mary care? Or should she make her decision solely on the basis of what the people of her own district—those who voted for her—would want her to do?

For the sake of this hypothetical case, let's say Mary concludes that health and ecological interests are, in general, more important than economic ones. On that basis, she decides that the public interest would be better served by the chemical company being refused permission to dump the chemical. Therefore, she turns down the company's request.

Interests in Conflict

Up to this point, we have given Mary a decision to make, a decision affecting both the public interest of the community at large and the private interests of various citizens within that community. Many of those interests conflict with one another: the interests of the workers in the chemical plant with those of the people who work in the fishing industry, for example. But so far there is no conflict of interest in the political sense. Mary has a public duty to perform, but she has no personal interest of her own.

In order to better understand conflicts of interest and the ethical problems they present for public officials, let's give Mary one.

Suppose that the situation is exactly the same, except that Mary discovers before she makes her decision that her grandfather has died and left her a great deal of stock in the chemical company. Now Mary has a direct economic interest in whether or not the company receives permission to dump. She can expect to profit financially if the company gets its permission, because her stock would go up in value. And she stands to suffer financially if that permission is refused, because her stock will go down.

Now a whole new factor must be added to the equations Mary must consider: her own financial stake in the decision.

Two main ethical dangers are raised by this kind of conflict of interest. The first is the temptation it offers for willful corruption. Mary might simply decide to use her public office for private gain. Despite her recognition that the public would be best served by her refusing to help the company, she might go ahead and help anyway, simply because she stands to profit if the company wins permission to dump waste in the river. Most politicians, it must be hoped, would not be so corrupt; they would not put their own financial interests above the health and safety of their constituents.

A second, more subtle ethical danger arises from such a conflict of interest. That danger has to do with the effects Mary's private interest might have on her judgment. Would the introduction of this new factor make a difference in Mary's analysis of the situation? Is her community of interest with the chemical company likely to make her more sympathetic to the arguments made by the company and less sympathetic to those made by its critics?

In this case, a group of scientists hired by the state described the ecological and public health results of dumping the chemical in the river. Those consequences were clear cut. Now let's suppose that the company hires scientists of its own who testify that the state's scientists are wrong. These new scientists argue that the damage would be much less than had been suggested. The chemical, they say, would kill only *some* of the fish, not all of them. True, the fishing industry would probably be hurt, but no more so than the chemical company would be hurt if it were denied permission to dump. Furthermore they testify that the chemical would probably never reach the groundwater, and therefore it would be unlikely to damage anyone's health.

Now Mary has to weigh the credibility (the reliability and believability) of the two groups of scientists. To which would she be likely to give more weight? Ordinarily, let's say, she would have relied more heavily on the state's scientists than on those hired by the company. She would have felt that, since the latter were employed by the company, they might be biased in its favor, and therefore discounted what they had to say. Will she be so likely to discount their evidence now that she has a common interest with them in the welfare of the company? Perhaps, but perhaps not.

The problem here is not which scientists are right and which are wrong. It is not even which decision would be the correct one for Mary to make. It is an ethical problem, but it concerns not so much her moral integrity as the integrity of her judgment. Even granting that Mary *wants* to make an ethical decision, can she do it?

Can Mary be as objective while owning stock in the company as she would have been without it? Can she judge the testimony of the scientists? Can she weigh the interests of the people of her district and those of the people of the state without the weight of her own financial interest tipping the scales?

Some people who want to ban all forms of conflict of interests would argue that she cannot. It is an accepted principle in disciplines as different as the law and medicine that one "cannot be objective in one's own case."

In the law, for example, there is a saying that "the lawyer who defends himself has a fool for a client." That is because to be effective a lawyer has to be able to view a case objectively. A lawyer would not be able to judge his or her own circumstances as clearly and objectively as another lawyer would. People cannot see themselves as others see them. An innocent defendant, for example, knowing himself to be innocent, could not fully understand how damaging evidence against him might seem to a jury.

The best of doctors have disregarded symptoms in themselves that any fellow doctor would immediately have recognized as serious, simply because they did not *want* them to be serious. Their own fear of sickness, and their desire to be well, colored their medical judgment.

The same kinds of circumstances can color the judgment of even the most conscientious public officials. It is often not so much a moral question as a psychological one. Politicians may try to be objective. They may not intend to put their private interests above their public duty. They may listen to the arguments on both sides of the issue and do their best to judge them fairly. But, say some observers, they cannot help being influenced by their own self-interest. They will naturally be biased in favor of those arguments that would promote their self-interest and against those that would damage it. In this, they are no different from lawyers or doctors or anyone else.

Others argue that it *is* possible for public officials to be objective, even when their own financial interests are involved. In fact, since some conflicts of interest are unavoidable, they have to be. Aside from the relatively few instances of willful corruption, conflicts of interest do not present a major ethical problem in American politics. If, in an individual case, certain public officials find it impossible to be objective, they can simply recuse themselves—they can refuse to act in that particular matter, allowing someone else to decide the issue. As long as the politicians involved are honorable and do not try to hide their financial interests from the public, these observers argue, there is little reason for concern.

For citizens, it comes down to an issue of trust. Can politicians be trusted to take actions in behalf of the public in matters where their private financial interests are involved?

What Can Be Done?

Although there is some disagreement about the extent of the ethical problem represented by conflicts of interest, there is general agreement in political circles that the problem exists and that steps should be taken to minimize it. Several such steps have been taken, by individual politicians and by political institutions alike.

A number of government bodies have established ethics offices where legislators or other public officials can go for advice on any ethical problems that arise. It may seem odd that elected officials should need a government office to help them make their ethical decisions. But one of the greatest problems presented by a conflict of interest is that it may interfere with an individual's ethical judgment.

The evidence clearly suggests that many politicians are badly in need of advice in these matters. When researchers asked 120 members of Congress to describe the conflicts of interest they had experienced, the researchers were surprised to find that the majority responded that they had never had a conflict of interest in their entire public lives! This seems highly unlikely, since some conflicts are unavoidable, as we have seen, and even the most honest members of Congress have certainly faced several of them in the course of their careers. The representatives who were questioned may have been reluctant to admit to something that might sound unethical to their constituents, or they may have simply failed to recognize those conflicts of interest that had occurred.

In any event, politicians use ethics offices for political protection as much as for ethical judgment. Acting on the advice of their ethics office gives them a defense against any future critics of their actions. The office's advice may or may not be any better than their own judgment would have been, but it is at least disinterested. Following it, officials can feel safe from any suggestion that they deliberately violated their public trust.

For the most part, efforts to do something about conflicts of interest have taken two forms: doing away with those conflicts that can be avoided, and disclosing those that remain.

On the federal level, both the House and the Senate have ethical codes for their members to follow. Among other things, these codes require members to limit their outside sources of income. The assumption is that by keeping their economic interests to a minimum, they will be keeping possible conflicts with those interests to a minimum as well.

Some public officials, particularly those who have large holdings of stocks and other investments, attempt to reduce potential conflicts by putting their investments into a "blind trust"—that is, they turn control of their financial affairs over to someone else while they are in public office. They themselves are kept in ignorance ("blind") about what happens to their investments. They are not even informed when stock is bought and sold for them. Because they don't know what their investments are, they cannot be tempted to use their office to enlarge them.

But the most important weapon in the struggle against conflicts of interest has been enforced disclosure. Both the House and Senate codes require members to file yearly reports revealing many details of their financial affairs. These include a list of all significant financial holdings and investments, as well as an accounting of how much money they received during the course of the year and where it came from. Similar disclosures are required of high officials in the executive branch of the federal government. Many states have disclosure requirements for state officials as well, although they are rarely as demanding as the federal codes.

Such disclosures do not do away with conflicts of interest, of course. But the reports, provided they are accurate, do reveal any conflicts to the voting public. The voters can then judge their representatives' records in the light of their financial interests. They can determine for themselves whether the politicians have allowed their private interests to interfere with their public duties.

Evidence suggests, however, that the disclosure requirements were not taken very seriously, at least at first. Many officials filed incomplete or misleading reports, and little was done to discipline the offenders. The disclosures remained largely unexamined by the press or public, anyway, and there was a tendency among politicians to become cavalier about them.

There are dangers in such an attitude, however, as the political world discovered in the presidential campaign of

1984. The incumbent Republican, Ronald Reagan, was expected to be a strong candidate for re-election. He was far ahead of the potential Democratic candidates in the public opinion polls. The eventual Democratic nominee, Walter Mondale, was not expected to have much of a chance to win the presidency *until* he took the historic step of choosing a woman, Congresswoman Geraldine Ferraro, as his vice presidential running mate.

Ferraro's nomination seemed to be a political masterstroke. She was an exciting and attractive candidate. Most important, she was a woman. Suddenly there was an excitement in the Mondale campaign that had been completely lacking before. Reagan's lead in the public opinion polls was all but wiped out overnight.

Then, just as suddenly as the excitement had been generated, the Democratic campaign went sour. Questions were raised about the financial disclosures Ferraro had made while serving in the House. It appeared that she had failed to disclose certain facts about her own and her husband's business dealings. There were strong suggestions of a hidden conflict of interest—that she had tried to hide a financial interest to disguise the fact that she was promoting that interest through votes in the House.

Ferraro did what she could to clarify her financial position. She explained that the flaws in the reports had been due to carelessness and not to any attempt to deceive the public. It eventually became clear that, far from promoting her supposedly secret financial interest, she had consistently voted against it. Although she was ultimately cleared of any illegality, a cloud of scandal had descended on the Mondale-Ferraro campaign that would never entirely lift. Reagan immediately jumped back to a big lead in the polls. When the election was held in November, he won forty-nine out of the fifty states.

The conflict-of-interest allegations made against Ferraro were not the only reason Reagan won, of course. He was personally popular, and it was generally believed that the

country had done well during his first term. But if the Democrats were to have had a chance to defeat him, they would have needed a big boost from the candidacy of Geraldine Ferraro. It seemed at first that they had gotten it. But the scandal over the misleading financial disclosures nullified that advantage almost immediately, and the Democratic presidential campaign never recovered.

Geraldine Ferraro, the 1984 Democratic vice-presidential candidate

7

*Betraying
the People's
Trust*

*Abusing
Public Office*

The obligations of political ethics do not stop when a politician is elected or appointed to office. If anything, they become heavier.

A public office is a public trust. In our political system, the government is the servant of the people. The individuals who work in government, whether at the local, state, or federal level, are public servants. They do what they do in behalf of the people, and the people have a right to expect that they will carry out their duties ethically.

In this respect, it does not matter if an officeholder is elected or appointed. Nor does it matter if he or she is the clerk of a sparsely populated rural county or the President of the United States. Whatever the office, and however it was obtained, the officeholder is obliged to perform his or her duties honestly and conscientiously. Not to do so is to abuse that office—and to betray the public trust.

Bribery

Perhaps the most clear-cut way in which elected officials sometimes betray their trust is by accepting bribes.

Bribery has a long history in American politics, dating back at least to 1795. That was the year of the nation's first big bribery scandal, known as the Yazoo land fraud. It was then revealed that four land companies had bribed enough members of the Georgia state legislature to induce the state to sell them a huge and immensely valuable tract of land. It included most of the area that now constitutes the states of Alabama and Mississippi. Bribery scandals have been a recurring theme in American political life ever since.

Any payment made to a public official in return for that official misusing his or her office is a bribe. The term covers a great many situations. It ranges from the "fixing" of a local parking ticket by a corrupt judge all the way up to such ambitious schemes as the Yazoo land fraud. Among notable examples of bribery that have come to light in the present century are the following:

In the 1920s, the Republican secretary of the interior, Albert Fall, leased the rights to drill oil on certain federal lands to friends, without competitive bidding. Those rights were estimated to be worth somewhere around $100 million. In return, Fall received large interest-free "loans" from his associates. He was eventually convicted of accepting bribes, although the men who had bribed him were acquitted.

In the 1960s, the secretary to the Democratic members of the Senate, Bobby Baker, was convicted on seven counts of tax evasion, one count of theft, and one count of conspiracy to defraud the government. Baker, a political associate of Lyndon Johnson, was an influential man. The trial revealed that he had, among other things, received over $99,000 from certain savings-and-loan institutions. Shortly thereafter, a $10 million tax increase that was to be levied on some of those institutions had been dropped.

In 1973, Republican Vice President of the United States Spiro Agnew was accused by his own administration's Justice Department of bribery and extortion, crimes the department said he had committed during his years as governor of Maryland. He resigned as vice president and pleaded *nolo contendere* to charges of income tax evasion—that is, while not admitting his guilt, he did not formally deny it. He was sentenced to three years' probation and a fine.

In the late 1970s, it was alleged that more than fifty congressmen—both House members and senators—had received money or other bribes from a South Korean businessman named Tongsun Park. Only a portion of the charges were ever proved, but the "Koreagate" scandal, as it came to be known, was more unnerving than most ordinary bribery scandals, because of its overtones of international intrigue. It was not merely that Park was a foreigner. He also had ties with the South Korean government, and it was suggested that the "gifts" had been given to promote not just his own business interests but his country's political interests as well. This raised the ominous possibility that a number of this country's elected officials had been acting secretly as agents of a foreign power.

In 1980, several congressmen as well as a number of state and local officials were caught in an FBI investigation nicknamed Abscam ("Arab scam"). FBI agents, having heard rumors that certain public officials were corrupt, posed as Arab sheikhs looking for favors. They approached the suspected officials and offered them bribes. Five Democratic congressmen and one Republican were among those who accepted money from the supposed sheikhs. The transactions were videotaped by a hidden television camera. The tapes were used at the resulting trials, and excerpts from them were shown on network television news programs. For the first time, the public got to see and hear some of its elected officials betraying their trust. As a result of Abscam,

Representative Michael O. "Ozzie" Myers became the first House member in history to be expelled from the House for corruption in office.

Bribes do not always come in the form of money. Sometimes, as we have already seen, they come in the form of help with a political campaign. Often, they are in the form of a noncash "gift."

Several members of the Truman administration in the 1940s were found to have accepted such "gifts" from businessmen for whom they'd done favors. Somewhat surprisingly, the gifts were primarily practical items such as home freezers, and only moderately expensive. An adviser to President Eisenhower in the following administration was revealed to have accepted a vicuña coat under similar circumstances. (A vicuña is a South American animal similar to a llama or an alpaca.)

Those officials were rank amateurs, however, compared to the really accomplished bribe takers of the time. Not long before their exposure, it was discovered that Senator Theodore Bilbo of Mississippi had accepted some really spectacular "gifts" in return for his services, which had also been spectacular. He had acquired some $25 million worth of defense contracts for business friends in Mississippi. In return, his friends had not only furnished his houses for him and presented him with a new car; they had also built him a swimming pool *and* an artificial lake!

Boodle

The proceeds of political corruption are called graft, or boodle. Bribery is an important source of these proceeds, but it is by no means the only one.

For many corrupt politicians, extortion can be even more profitable. Extortion is a kind of enforced bribery. The public official, in effect, *demands* a bribe. Sometimes the demand is made in return for doing a favor. Often it is

"SAM, HERE, IS IN CHARGE OF ETHICS. HE SEES
THAT WE DON'T PAY OUT MORE IN BRIBES
THAN WE RECEIVE IN KICKBACKS."

made in return for *not* doing something. Police officers, for example, have been known to extort payments from criminals by threatening to arrest them if they do not pay.

Even honest citizens can have money extorted from them by dishonest officials. City officials in charge of granting business licenses, for example, have been known to extort payments from applicants before considering them for a license.

"Padding" expense accounts is another source of dishonest funds. Officials claim that they have incurred higher expenses in the course of their duties than they have. When the government reimburses them the full amount of their claim, they pocket the difference as boodle.

Still another source of boodle is the kickback. Like extortion, the kickback comes in several forms. One of the most common is that demanded by unethical officials from businesses that supply the government with goods and services. An official with the authority to make purchases of goods or services for the government allows suppliers to overcharge—as long as a portion of the extra cost is "kicked back" to the official as boodle.

Some officials are entitled to hire staff members to help them with their work. A state senator, say, might be able to hire a secretary at the state government's expense. An important federal official might be able to hire a large staff of secretaries, researchers, and other assistants. For unethical politicians, having jobs at their disposal can be a continuing source of boodle. Employees are hired on the understanding that they will kick back a portion of each paycheck to their boss. For the public official with a number of jobs to offer, kickbacks can be an extremely lucrative source of income.

It isn't known how widespread this practice actually is, since such payments are secret, but every now and then an example of it comes to light. In 1978, for example, Charles C. Diggs, a Democratic congressman from Michigan, was convicted of taking kickbacks from members of his congressional staff.

Two years before Diggs's conviction, it was revealed that one of his fellow congressmen had put a government job to still another kind of unethical use. Elizabeth Ray, a secretary employed by a committee under his control, accused Representative Wayne Hays of putting her on the government payroll as a way of paying her for being his mistress. Supporting her charge, Ray pointed out that she "couldn't even type." Hays, who had been one of the most powerful men in Washington, was forced to resign from the House.

More than a few politicians have regarded the public payroll as a kind of family employment service, using it to provide jobs for members of their immediate family or other relatives. This practice of favoring one's relatives is called nepotism.

Some people argue that giving a job, even a public job, to a relative is not necessarily unethical. If the relative is qualified to perform a government job, why shouldn't he or she get it?

Opponents of the practice argue that nepotism is often nothing more than a way of doing relatives favors with tax-payers' money. Even when the relative seems to be qualified, the suspicion lingers that he or she was hired only because of family ties to the politician, which would be unfair to all the other applicants for the job. When public money is being spent to provide a job, opponents feel, all citizens should have an equal opportunity to apply for it. No one should receive favored treatment because of family relationships.

These are only some of the forms that boodle takes. There are many others. For the public official who is both enterprising and corrupt, the opportunities for personal wealth are virtually unlimited. Two celebrated examples will demonstrate this: Thomas J. Farley, whose salary as sheriff of New York County ranged between $6,500 and $15,000 a year during six years in office, managed to deposit some $396,000 in his personal bank account during that time. Richard Leche, whose salary as governor of Louisiana was a mere $7,500 a year, used it to generate over $250,000 in boodle in a single year. And both of these financial feats were accomplished in the 1930s, when the dollar was worth a great deal more than it is today.

The Machines

The true masters of boodle were the bosses who ran the corrupt political machines that flourished in the nineteenth and early twentieth centuries.

The object of the machines was to control the government of their city or region by controlling access to public office and public jobs.

Machines were the children of two other political institutions: the political party and the patronage system. Most of them started out, in fact, as local or state party organizations. (In a sense, both the Republican and Democratic parties are "machines." But on the national level, at least, they have traditionally been too divided and undisciplined to fully deserve that title.) Having established themselves, usually under the control of a local boss or alliance of bosses, they continued to operate as chapters of the national party, supplying it with candidates for local and state office and with sure votes for the party's national candidates.

The machine's power depended on its ability to control the election process within its own territory. In some places, this was relatively easy to do. The populations were so heavily Republican or Democratic that a majority vote for a particular party was virtually automatic. Sometimes it was more difficult. At those times, many machines turned to unethical practices to ensure that their candidates would be elected.

The machines maintained their power by using the spoils system, or patronage, their control of government jobs. Once the machine got charge of a city, county, or state government, it determined which people that government would hire. In some jurisdictions, that meant control of thousands and thousands of jobs. The machine used those jobs to reward those party workers who helped keep the machine in power, and it made sure that no one hostile to it could ever work for the government or ever be elected to public office. This was an essential element of the machine's power. The bosses decided who the candidates would be and what office they would hold. This meant, of course, that the people were never given a real choice. As one of the most powerful of all the bosses, William Marcy Tweed of New York's Democratic machine, Tammany Hall, put it in the nineteenth century: "You may elect whichever candidate you please to office—if you will allow me to select the candidates."

Many of the machines financed themselves with public funds. They required the government employees they'd hired to kick back some of their salaries to the party; and they awarded government contracts to businessmen at unnecessarily high costs to the taxpayers, expecting a certain amount of the money to be kicked back.

One of the most unsavory aspects of the machines was the ties many of them had to organized crime and vice. Machine politics often went hand in hand not only with political bribery and extortion but with other forms of crime as well. In many big cities, payoffs to the local bosses could assure a bookmaker, prostitution ring, or other illegal operation that it would be able to function without having to worry about the law.

A political organization did not have to be corrupt in order to qualify as a machine, but most machines were corrupt to one degree or another. The reason was simple: it was easier, and more profitable, that way.

For much of the nation's history—certainly from 1800 to the 1960s—most big cities had at least one powerful political machine. In cities in which Democrats predominated, it would be Democratic. In Republican cities, it would be Republican. In some areas, where there were large numbers of both Democrats and Republicans, there would be two machines. Sometimes they would compete for power, and when they did, the competition could be vicious. Sometimes, however, they would collaborate, agreeing between themselves which political offices would be controlled by one machine, which by the other. In that way, each kept a certain amount of power and a certain number of jobs at its disposal, and neither risked being destroyed by the other.

It was not just the big cities that had machines. Rural areas, too, were subject to machine rule. As we have already seen, a political machine in rural Texas helped elect Lyndon Johnson to the Senate.

In general, the machines prospered best in areas with large numbers of immigrants: Irish, Italians, Germans, and other Europeans in the larger cities; Mexicans in the rural Southwest. Immigrants provided good material for the machines. The members of each ethnic group tended to gather together, which made them easier to manipulate. They were close-knit and liked to do things together, including taking part in political activities. Each immigrant community had leaders who could be taken into the machine, bringing the votes of their fellows with them. The machines took the immigrants under their wings, instructed them in the ways of their new country, including supporting the machine, looked after their political interests, gave many of them jobs, and provided various kinds of help for those who were in need. In return, they expected political loyalty. And they got it.

Although machines were usually local or, at the most, statewide organizations, they had national significance. As has already been mentioned, they were allied with the national political parties. Since they controlled large numbers of votes, they often had major, and sometimes decisive, effects on national elections.

For most of the country's history, few men, if any, were elected President of the United States without the cooperation and support of one or more of the machines. When one President, Benjamin Harrison, gave Providence the credit for his election, the Republican boss of Pennsylvania, Matthew Quay, was offended. It wasn't Providence that had won Harrison the presidency, Quay snorted. The credit belonged to himself and the other Republican bosses. And, said Quay, they had "approached the gates of the penitentiary" in order to do it.

Harrison had been an unknowing beneficiary of machine support. Other national leaders were products of local machines themselves. Among them were some Presidents, including Harry S Truman, who was a protégé of Tom Pendergast, the Democratic boss of Kansas City, Missouri.

For some years now, the machines have been in decline. A number of circumstances have combined to erode their power. Their ability to handpick candidates has been destroyed by the greater use of the party primary, in which the voters choose their own candidates. The immigrants who were once so essential to the machines have been replaced by new generations of people who have grown up in this country and who don't need the help of the machines. Many of the jobs that used to be at the disposal of political officials are now awarded through objective tests and are no longer available for patronage. Many of the social services that the machines used to provide to their supporters are now provided to all citizens by the state and federal governments.

Perhaps most important, the kind of raw political corruption the machines represented has become unacceptable to a better informed, more politically active electorate.

Misusing Government for Public Aims

The abuses of office we have discussed so far have been carried out largely for personal gain. But there are other kinds of abuse of office as well—abuses committed for what the abusers see as the public good.

One of the most common of these practices is deliberately misleading the public about what the government is doing. In wartime, for example, the government has often been known to hide a defeat or inflate the importance of a victory in order to keep up morale at home. When a President has been ill, that fact has sometimes been hidden in order to keep the President, or even the country, from seeming weak.

When officials mislead the public in this way, they are usually convinced that they are doing so for the good of the country. They forget that in a democratic system it is up to the people to decide what is good for the country, and that the people can't do that without knowing the truth.

Some of the most ironic abuses of office are those related to law enforcement. In these cases, it is the very people who are supposed to uphold the law who break it, and they do so in the name of law and order. Such abuses are ironic enough on the local level, when city police violate citizens' constitutional rights. They are even more so at the federal level, when powerful agencies such as the FBI, the CIA, and the Justice Department do so.

Under its longtime chief, J. Edgar Hoover, the FBI made a regular practice of violating the rights of citizens Hoover believed to be "subversive" or "dangerous." Agents harassed large numbers of people who were never even accused of a crime. The FBI tapped their phones, followed them openly, searched their homes secretly without a legal warrant, and carried out many other kinds of illegal activities against them.

These kinds of activities on the part of the FBI reached their most extreme form in the 1960s. At that time, Hoover believed that the civil rights and anti-war movements threatened the security of the United States, and the FBI resorted to many illegal practices in its effort to counter the threat.

"The Hanging Tree"

The agency infiltrated peace groups, women's rights organizations, and even politically active church groups. Members of the Bureau, or others working for it, often acted as *agents provocateurs*, encouraging law-abiding groups to commit crimes so that law enforcement agencies would have an excuse to crack down on them. The agency launched smear campaigns to discredit the leaders of such groups. It spread false stories about them—not just about their political activities but about their sexual practices as well.

Nor did it stop with destroying their public reputations. It tried to disrupt their personal lives by getting them fired from their jobs and even sending their spouses anonymous letters suggesting they were being unfaithful. Probably the most notorious of all these campaigns was the one directed against the civil rights leader Martin Luther King, Jr., whom Hoover seemed to hate. An FBI report referred to the eventual Nobel Peace Prize winner, who has since had a national holiday declared in his honor, as "the most dangerous . . . Negro leader in the country."

The CIA (Central Intelligence Agency) is another federal agency that has sometimes been accused of misusing its powers. The CIA was intended primarily as a gatherer of intelligence information from foreign countries. It was forbidden to act within the United States itself, or to spy on American citizens. But members of the Agency have admitted that it did just that for many years, collecting personal information on at least ten thousand American citizens. For decades, it also opened and read the mail of many Americans, a violation of their fundamental rights.

In its foreign operations, too, the CIA regularly violated commonly understood ethical principles. It carried out experiments with dangerous drugs on people who had no idea they were being used as guinea pigs; and it took part in attempts to murder foreign leaders—at least once in cooperation with members of the Mafia.

"WHERE BUT IN AMERICA COULD A POOR FARM BOY WORK
HIS WAY UP, IN FOUR SHORT YEARS, TO BECOME THE
HEAD OF A SMALL BUT IMPORTANT FOREIGN COUNTRY?"

In the mid-1970s, following a fifteen-month investigation of such illegal activities by federal agencies, the Select Committee on Intelligence of the U.S. Senate came to a shocking conclusion. For several decades, extending through both Republican and Democratic administrations in Washington, the FBI and CIA, among other government agencies, had been operating "outside the law."

These are just some of the many ways in which officials and agencies have abused their trust in the name of the public good. In all these cases, the abusers felt that they were in the right. If they were asked, they would say that they had acted to protect America and its ideals of freedom and democracy. They clearly feel that in cases such as these, the ends at least partly justify the means. They believe that their noble motives somehow serve as an excuse for their actions.

Defenders of the FBI and CIA would emphasize the importance and difficulty of the agencies' jobs. They are responsible for fighting terrorists and the agents of hostile foreign powers. They are protecting not just individual citizens but the country itself. The criminals they oppose have no respect for the law, but only use it to hide behind. The methods described above seem unethical, but when fighting enemies as ruthless as those faced by these government agencies, they are both necessary and justified.

Critics of the agencies, however, respond that the nobility of the agencies' motives in no way excuses their abusive methods. To some extent, they say, these abuses of office are ethically even worse than those carried out for personal gain. When public officials deceive the public, violate constitutional rights, commit burglaries, and even plan murders—all in the name of protecting American ideals—those ideals are not just violated, they are destroyed.

Private Morality and Public Office

Questions are often raised about the ethical behavior of politicians in areas not related to their political roles.

Charges of scandalous personal behavior have been a staple of American political life from the beginning of the nation. Such charges have been hurled at politicians on every level of government, including Presidents of the United States, and they have involved virtually every aspect of their private lives and moral characters.

Sexual misconduct has long been a popular subject for scandal. Our third President, Thomas Jefferson, was accused by the Federalists of having fathered five illegitimate children by Sally Hemings, one of his black slaves. It was an indication of the times that it was not *owning* Sally Hemings that counted against him but having children with her, even though the alleged relationship between the two was said to have been mutually loving. Several decades later, in 1884, the Republicans accused the Democratic presidential candidate, Grover Cleveland, of having fathered an illegitimate child, ridiculing him publicly with the mocking chant: "Ma, Ma, where's my pa? Gone to the White House, ha, ha, ha."

Drunkenness is another popular charge. Both Jefferson and Cleveland were among the Presidents who were accused of it, as was Ulysses S. Grant. The charge against Grant first came up while he served as the commanding general of Union forces during the Civil War. When President Lincoln was told that his favorite general was a drunk, he made a famous joke. Considering how well Grant was performing in the field, Lincoln said he'd like to know what brand of liquor he was drinking so he could send some to all his generals.

Other subjects for scandal include charges of drug abuse, criminal behavior, and personal financial irregularities unrelated to the politician's public service.

These charges are of a different kind from those we described earlier. The earlier examples had to do with questions of *public* morality and unethical *political* behavior —in other words, with what politicians do *as* politicians, either while running for public office or serving in it. These new examples, on the other hand, have to do with *private* morality and unethical *personal* behavior—with what politicians do as private citizens.

Some politicians would argue that such things have nothing to do with political ethics at all. They are private matters and should be kept out of the political arena. What politicians do in their bedrooms has no bearing on whether or not they should hold public office. Neither does what or how much they drink, so long as they never let drunkenness interfere with their public duties.

According to this argument, private vices of any kind are irrelevant to a politician's qualifications for office. After all, as we have seen, some of the greatest figures in our history have been accused of such vices. Did the personal moral frailties of Ulysses S. Grant and Thomas Jefferson disqualify them? Would the Union have been better off without its most victorious general because he was said to drink too much? Would the nation have been better off without the services of one of its most influential Founding Fathers—the man who wrote the Declaration of Independence—because he may have had illicit sexual relations with a slave?

But others believe that *any* kind of immoral behavior is relevant to a politician's qualifications for office. They believe that all parts of a person's moral character are connected. A person who is unethical in one area of life is likely to be unethical in other areas as well. A politician who cannot resist the temptation to take a drink may not be able to resist the temptation to take a bribe either. A man who is unfaithful to his wife cannot be trusted to be faithful to his public duties.

Those arguments, however, seem to be disproven by a number of cases, including that of Jefferson.

Still, some observers believe that a public servant owes the public a decent and moral life in all areas, not just in the performance of his or her office. They believe citizens have a right to look to their public officials for a good example. To them, personal immorality is still another form of abusing the public trust.

The Watergate Scandal

The most wide-ranging examples of abuse of the public trust in recent history were revealed in what has come to be known as the Watergate scandal, which occurred in the presidential administration of Richard Nixon. It began with a variety of unethical campaign practices and ended with the resignation, in disgrace, of the President of the United States.

Richard Nixon had been elected in a close race in 1968. By 1972, he had established himself as a respected and widely admired President. When the Democrats nominated the liberal senator George McGovern to run against him in that year's election, it seemed virtually certain that Nixon would win re-election. McGovern was perceived by most observers as too far to the political left to satisfy most voters.

Nonetheless, the people in Nixon's campaign resorted to an incredible variety of unethical and even illegal tactics to ensure the President's re-election. Some of these, Donald Segretti's dirty tricks, have already been described. But they were far from the most controversial acts engaged in by Nixon's Committee to Re-Elect the President, commonly known by its acronym, CREEP. Among other criminal acts, people working for the committee broke into the headquarters of the Democratic National Committee in the Watergate building in Washington, D.C. Once inside, they photographed private documents and planted "bugs" (secret microphones) that let them listen to the Democrats' private conversations. Before they could escape, they were caught.

The burglars' guilty connection to CREEP was not fully established, however, until after the election, and by then Nixon had been returned to office by a large margin. Over the next several months, the scandal set off by the burglary at the Watergate finally broke out.

Investigations by some members of the press, and finally by House and Senate committees, revealed a wide range of corruption and abuse of power within the Nixon administration. Over the previous four years, the administration had kept a political enemies list of citizens whose only crime was having opposed Richard Nixon's policies. Administration employees asked the Internal Revenue Service and other government agencies to harass these "enemies." Secret money had been demanded from wealthy contributors. The offices of a psychiatrist had been illegally broken into in order to find damaging information about one of his patients. The list of abuses seemed endless.

As the facts began to come out, Nixon and his people did everything they could to hide them. The President himself went on national television and lied about what he had done. The White House offered blackmail money to the jailed burglars in order to buy their silence. The President's close friends and advisers committed perjury to avoid having the truth about their campaign activities become public.

Eventually the truth *did* become public, of course. Nixon was forced to resign from the presidency when it became clear that Congress was about to impeach him. Many of his political friends—including some of the highest-ranking officials in the federal government—went to jail. Nixon himself escaped possible imprisonment only by receiving an unconditional pardon from Gerald Ford, the man he had made President by his resignation.

The pardon itself gave rise to charges of corruption. To some, it suggested an implied "deal." Perhaps Nixon had, in effect, made Ford President in return for a promise that Ford would pardon him if it became necessary. There was no direct proof of these suspicions, but many Americans, already made cynical by the Watergate revelations, were extremely suspicious of the pardon. Several political experts blame the pardon for the fact that Ford, who was otherwise well liked by the public at large, lost his effort to win the presidency for himself in 1976.

Some of the most interesting aspects of the Watergate

scandal, aside from the sheer scope of it, are the justifications offered by the participants for their actions. Various members of the administration claimed that many of their actions had been carried out in the interests of "national security," in order to protect the country. When these men were closely questioned by Senator Sam Ervin and others, it became clear that many of them saw the continuation of the Nixon administration as being in the national interest. A McGovern administration, as they saw it, would have been bad for the nation. Therefore, any actions they took to defeat McGovern and re-elect Nixon were, in their opinion, justified as being for the good of the country. They identified Nixon's (and their own) political ambitions with the welfare of the United States. What was good for Richard Nixon was good for the country. It was only a step from that proposition to the proposition that any enemy of Richard Nixon's was an enemy of the country. And from there to the enemies list.

Another argument some of them raised in their defense was that the President is above the law. Since the President is the chief executive officer of the land, he cannot be guilty of a crime. The proposition was rejected by most legal experts, but many of Nixon's supporters believed it.

Still others, among them some who were convicted of crimes and sent to jail, argued strongly that they had acted out of duty. The President was their Commander in Chief and, as good soldiers, it was their duty to obey his orders whatever they might personally think of them. In their minds, they had acted ethically. To them, loyalty and obedience to the President were higher values than the law and the Constitution of the United States.

Richard M. Nixon after he resigned the presidency in 1974

*Assessing
the Damage*

Political Theft

One way to understand the damage done by the unethical practices described in this book is to look at them as forms of theft. Just as there are different kinds of ordinary robberies—burglaries, muggings, holdups, and so forth—there are different kinds of political theft. Some of them are as simple and direct as any street crime. Take extortion, for example.

Ethically it matters very little whether money is extorted by a government official in the form of a kickback from an employee's salary, demanded in return for a tavern license, or taken at the point of a gun in the street. It is all theft.

When government jobs are handed out as patronage in return for political loyalty to a given party or official, they are in a sense stolen from those potentially more deserving workers who are robbed of any chance to be considered for them.

When an officeholder takes a bribe to do a favor for one citizen, or one group of citizens, that favor is invariably done at the expense of someone else. If the favor is a government contract, for example, why shouldn't other companies have a fair chance to bid for it? Another company might do the job for the government better and cheaper. If so, the bribe not only robs that company of a contract; it also robs the public of a more efficient government contractor.

Most bribes end up being paid at the expense of the public at large. Government money—money taken from all tax-paying citizens, presumably for public purposes—is handed over to corrupt private individuals or corporations.

Those who commit some forms of political robbery steal things that might be considered more important than money. When political machines handpick the candidates who can run for office, the voters are robbed of a free choice.

When a candidate wins an election through fraud of any kind—whether by misrepresenting the truth, by dirty tricks, by buying votes, by intimidating voters, or by tampering with ballots and voting machines—that, too, is a form of robbery. And a stolen election robs not just the opposing candidates but the public as well. The people are robbed of one of their most fundamental political rights: the right to choose their representatives in government.

When special interests monopolize the attention of our elected officials through the power of their money and their organization, that can be considered still another form of robbery. Every citizen has a right to petition the government, to be heard, and to be considered. But when the scales are so weighted in favor of the organized—in favor of the PACs and their lobbyists—the "politics of intimidation" takes over, and the voice of the individual citizen is lost.

In all of these cases, both private individuals and the society itself are robbed—robbed of a free and ethical political system.

There is no way to tell how widespread any of these practices actually are. The only examples we hear about, such as the ones mentioned in this book, are those where the secrecy in which they are usually carried out has somehow broken down. But these are only a small sampling of the cases that have become public knowledge, and it is impossible to say how many cases remain secret for every one that has been exposed.

It would be a mistake, then, to assume that all political corruption has been exposed, or to assume that political corruption is a thing of the past. Corruption has been a fact of political life throughout history, and there is no reason to believe that politicians are any more honest or honorable today than they have ever been.

At the same time, it would be a mistake to assume that they are any *less* honorable than they have ever been, or that corruption is universal among them. It is not. There is no evidence to indicate that politicians as a group are any more corrupt than people in other walks of life. There is probably at least as high a proportion of corruption in business, finance, medicine, sports, and most other professions as there is in politics.

Both mistakes—assuming that almost no present-day politicians are corrupt, and assuming that all of them are— seem to be common among the American electorate. At times, these conflicting assumptions are held simultaneously. There is a real ambivalence in the public's attitude toward politicians.

That ambivalence shows up in many ways. When people are asked in public opinion polls what they think about the ethics of American politicians, they are apt to give two very different answers. When asked about politicians *in general*, they often say they believe most of them to be corrupt or incompetent, or both. But when asked about their *own* politicians—the ones whom they voted for, and who represent them at all levels of government—they usually answer that they believe them to be both honest and capable.

This ambivalence shows itself in the public's responses to political scandals. The public opposes corruption in general but is often surprisingly tolerant of it in specific cases.

Time and time again, officeholders have been re-elected despite scandals that showed them to be unethical. A notable instance of this was the case of Congressman Adam Clayton Powell, Jr. Powell, a Democrat, was censured by the House in 1967 for gross financial misdealings and other abuses. His offenses were so extravagant that the House voted to exclude him from membership. In his own district in New York City's Harlem, however, Powell was a hero, largely because of his many valiant battles for civil rights. Despite his blatant misdeeds, his constituents immediately re-elected him and sent him back to the House which had rejected him. (The Supreme Court later ruled that the House's vote to exclude him had been unconstitutional.) Powell's case was extreme, but it was not unique. Politicians have even been re-elected to office while serving time in prison for abusing their office.

Voters have sometimes shown themselves tolerant of other forms of unethical behavior as well. In 1983, for example, two congressmen, Dan Crane and Gerry Studds, were involved in similar sex scandals. Crane, a married Republican from Rhode Island, had had sexual relations with a seventeen-year-old female congressional page, while Studds, a Democrat from Massachusetts, had engaged in sexual relations with a male page of the same age. Both men were accused of illicit sexual relations with young people and of abusing their position as congressmen by taking advantage of congressional employees. Crane publicly apologized, while Studds, arguing that the relationship had been mutually consenting, refused to apologize. Both men were censured by the House, but both were later re-elected by their constituents.

It is difficult to say just what this voter tolerance means. In some cases, no doubt, it reflects a feeling on the part of constituents that their representatives were dealt with unfairly, that the media were too hard on them, and that the public scandal was punishment enough for what they had done. In other instances, voters seem to feel that a given politician is so effective at representing them that they are willing to put up with a certain amount of unethical conduct rather than lose his or her services. In still other cases—particularly those of offenders like Theodore Bilbo, Adam Clayton Powell, Jr., and many of the old-time big-city bosses—the voters seem to positively enjoy hearing about the dishonest exploits of their politicians.

Sometimes the level of the voters' tolerance depends on their political compatibility with the politician in question. When Richard Nixon was forced to resign from the presidency as a result of the Watergate scandal, some Republicans who had been strong supporters of the President felt that he should have been allowed to remain in office. They argued that the Watergate affair had been blown out of proportion by a hostile press. What is more, they argued that the allegations against the President—which included accepting illegal campaign contributions, encouraging perjury, presiding over a massive governmental cover-up of criminal activities, and deliberately lying to the American people—were really quite minor. Besides, they complained, Nixon had not done anything that his Democratic predecessors in office had not done as well. Perhaps what Nixon had done was wrong, but it didn't warrant kicking him out of office. Only a relatively few Republicans took that view, however, and virtually no Democrats did.

The great majority of those willing to overlook Nixon's offenses were people who had long supported the President on other matters. Their attitude toward this matter, so different from the ethical judgment of most Americans, seems to be most logically explained by their overall political views. Their belief that Nixon had been a good President in most respects colored their judgment of the seriousness of what he had done.

Although voters sometimes show a great deal of tolerance for unethical political behavior, at other times they show none at all. Many officials have been turned out of office at the first sign of corruption. In the next election following the Abscam revelations, for example, all the guilty congressmen who ran for re-election were defeated.

Even tolerant voters rarely remain tolerant forever in the face of repeated abuses. Except in those cases in which a machine has been powerful enough to completely control all election results, most politicians who have repeatedly been shown to be corrupt have eventually been rejected by their constituents. Even Adam Clayton Powell, Jr., was finally defeated for re-election in 1970.

Although many voters claim to be cynical about the ethics of politicians in general, and although they may be surprisingly tolerant of the ethical failures of those politicians they like, the evidence suggests that they do care about the moral qualities of the men and women they elect to public office. They do expect them to behave honorably. And they will ultimately hold them to the standards of conduct and moral judgment that are the essence of political ethics.

Why We Should Care

It is vital that we hold our politicians to such an ethical standard.

At the same time, it is also necessary not to set that standard unrealistically high. The world of politics is a world of conflicts. Part of the job of a politician is to resolve those conflicts. In a democracy, that job requires compromise—between competing groups and interests and some-

"THEY JUST DON'T MAKE PRESIDENTS
LIKE THEY USED TO."

times between competing values and principles as well. There is often a very narrow line between compromise and corruption. Any usable standard of political ethics must recognize that line. It must not mistake the one for the other, and it must not be set so high as to make compromise impossible.

All too often, however, compromise *does* slip over the line into ethical misconduct, into corruption. The standard must be set high enough not to allow that.

Such a standard, and the willingness to hold our politicians to it, is vital to the health of our political system. The greatest harm that can be done to that system is not the damage done by the corrupt actions of individual politicians. It is the loss of faith in the system that we suffer when we, the people of this country, condone those corrupt actions. When we tolerate corruption as an unavoidable element of the political process, we allow not just the individual politicians but the system itself to become corrupt.

Finally, the most important reason we must refuse to tolerate political corruption lies in the representative nature of our political system. Unlike the citizens of some countries, who bear little or no responsibility for the actions of their governments, we are implicated in what our government does. Our political officials act in our name, with our expressed consent. They are not just our leaders; they are our representatives. In a very real sense, what they do, we do.

Ultimately, their ethics are our ethics. If they are corrupt, and we allow them to be, then we are corrupt, too. All citizens must be concerned about that.

Suggested Reading

Politics, both honest and corrupt, has proved to be a rich source for literature of all kinds. Many books are available on virtually every subject touched on in this one. The following is just a sampling. A trip to the card catalog of your local or school library will yield many more.

*On campaign financing
and its effects on politics:*

Adamany, David W., and George E. Agree. *Political Money: A Strategy for Campaign Financing in America.* Baltimore: Johns Hopkins University Press, 1975.

Alexander, Herbert E. *Money in Politics.* Washington, D.C.: Public Affairs Press, 1972.

Etzioni, Amitai. *Capital Corruption, the New Attack on American Democracy.* San Diego: Harcourt Brace Jovanovich, 1984.

Thayer, George. *Who Shakes the Money Tree? American Campaign Financing Practices from 1789 to the Present.* New York: Simon & Schuster, 1973.

*On the man who has been called
"the last of the big city bosses":*

Kennedy, Eugene. *Himself! The Life and Times of Mayor Richard J. Daley.* New York: Viking Press, 1978.

*Finally, for a look at the political
ethics of all our Presidents from
George Washington through
Jimmy Carter:*

Bailey, Thomas A. *Presidential Saints and Sinners.* New York: Free Press, 1981.

Index

About
the
Author

Michael Kronenwetter is a free-lance writer who wears many hats. He is a newspaper columnist and media critic who has also written award-winning filmstrips and radio plays.

Mr. Kronenwetter attended Northwestern University and the University of Wisconsin. His books include a history of the region of central Wisconsin where he was raised and now makes his home, and three other books for Franklin Watts: *Are You a Liberal? Are You a Conservative?* and *Free Press v. Fair Trial: Television and Other Media in the Courtroom*, and *Capitalism vs. Socialism.*